Decoding Ṛig-Veda

For the Knowledge of Science

Radhika Raman Prasad Sinha

Decoding Ṛig-Veda
For the Knowledge of Science

ISBN: 978-1-935125-22-8

Printed in the United States of America

To order additional books go to:

www.RP-Author.com/Sinha

Cover Concept

Aerial photograph prior to Sunrise (Usha), at the Pacific Ocean. The inset "...blazing fire on Aryan altar," is a condensed image of the same.

The rising Sun improves eyesight and tones up heart and mind. This period of Usha is for growth and expansion of energy, intellect and all that is good for human health. This hour is called Brahm Bela, meaning the hour of Brahma.

Photo credit: Anoop Sharma

Formatted and submitted for publication by:
Prabhakar Aloka, Amitabh Divakar, and Binita Sinha-Sharma

Contact:

Prabhakar Aloka: praloka@gmail.com
Amitabh Divakar: amitabhdivakar@hotmail.com
Binita Sinha-Sharma: bsinha@msn.com

Robertson Publishing
59 N. Santa Cruz Avenue, Suite B
Los Gatos, California 95030 USA
(888) 354-5957 • www.RobertsonPublishing.com

Dedicated to the coming generations of erudite scientists, discoverers and inventors who would like to decode the hymns of Ṛig-Veda for finding out truths not yet understood and to utilize those truths for the sake of humanity in general.

Table of Contents

Title .... Page Number

About the Author v

My Regards vii

Salutations to Guru ix

Preface xi

What is Veda 1

Nature 9

Rishi 11

Gods and Goddesses 19-89

- Brahma, Vishnu, Mahesh 19
- Aditi 21
- Agni 23
- Indra 29
- Aswini Kumars 36
- Som 44
- Surya 54
- Chandra 61
- Brihaspati 62
- Rudra 65
- Ribhus 68
- Etasha 71

Table of Contents (contd.)

Title .... Page Number

- Vayu 73
- Saraswati 75
- Ila 76
- Bharati 76
- Urvashi 77
- Rati 78
- Raka 79
- Ratri 79
- Usha 80
- Dakshina 85
- Sarma 86

Creation 91

Conclusion 97

Appendix 103-134

- A - Vritra 103
- B - Moon 105
- C - Pusa 107
- D - Kamdeo 109
- E - Aswin Kumars 111
- F - Daksha 113
- G - Adityas 119
- H - Jyotish Shashtra 121
- I - Metres 125
- J - Various types of Marriages 129
- K - Brahma's Day and Night 131
- L - Pioneers in Science and Technology 135

Bibliography 137

About the Author

Radhika Raman Prasad Sinha was born on May 26, 1937, at old Patna City in the vicinity of Patna Sahib Gurudwara in the Bihar state, India. The eldest son of Sri. Gorakh Prasad and Smt. Umraoti Devi, he spent his childhood with maternal and paternal grandparents and extended family. Received his early education in Daltonganj, Bihar. After completing post-secondary education from St. Xaviers College, Ranchi, joined the Bihar Institute of Technology, Sindri, and specialized in electrical engineering. Received his Guru Diksha at the age of eighteen and after completing his studies at a young age of twenty-one, taught at Patna Engineering College before joining the State Electricity Board. Retired in 1996 as General Manager-cum-Chief engineer of Patna Electric Supply Undertaking (PESU).

He had deep love and respect for natures' creations and enjoyed travelling. One of his reports "Bhimbandh : A Paradise Undiscovered", extensively documented the natural hot-springs of Bhimbandh in eastern Bihar. As a hobby, he also studied astrology with an objective of finding correlation between planetary positions in ones horoscope and health.

It was his quest for scientific meaning behind rituals and customs that eventually led him to an in-depth study of the ancient Indian scriptures particularly the Vedas. He spent his post-retirement period in Patna researching the Vedas.

He left for heavenly abode at dusk (Godhuli Bela) sitting on his 'asana' at his favorite spot in the garden on March 2, 2008. He is survived by his wife Mrs. Vidya Sinha, two sons, daughter-in-law, daughter, son-in-law, and two grandsons. This book is published posthumously based on the manuscript he had completed.

My Regards

At the outset I pay regards to those scholars of modern science and technology who say that there is no trace of science and technology in the books of Vedas. Words like telephone, computer, locomotive, do not find place in the Vedas nor is there mention of formulae, calculus, or differential equations. Most of us have very limited knowledge of the old Sanskrit literature. And also we have little knowledge of coding of Sanskrit words for the sake of secrecy or brevity.

The verses or hymns of the first book of Vedas – the Ṛig-Veda, are for singing. The observers, the seers of thought, the Rishis, pure in heart and mind and with elevated consciousness had heard the whispers of nature and presented it in the form of music in common language for a common man even though the verses have deep meanings for erudite persons and researchers.

The ellipsoidal orbit and shape of the earth are much recent discovery of modern science through the works of Kepler and Newton, but the Rishis of Vedic period had already observed it. Also, they observed the universe to be expanding.

Now, scientists talk of the Big Bang theory. The ancient observers noted similar phenomena in a different manner. They had the ability to make precise calculations. The ancients knew what is known to the modern science but modern science does not know everything that was known to the ancients.

Science scholars as well as students of science along with scholars of Sanskrit can work together and decode the book of Ṛig-Veda which stores immense knowledge, large and deep like the Pacific Ocean. Just like the Ṛig-Veda, other books of the Veda namely, Yajur-Veda, Atharwa-Veda, and Sam-Veda also should be decoded.

Scholars and students of science should follow what Max Muller has advised. He said that no single mind can understand the Vedas. If scholars of different faculties of science and Sanskrit sit together then the observations of the Vedas can be understood.

At last, the request is that women and children should not be deprived of the opportunity of reading the Vedas. Among ancient observers of the Vedic period there were thirty women. In fact, women have more intuitive capabilities. A kid's mind is pure and closer to truth. Little Aishwarya asked whether any of the Rishis desired for a daughter. Another kid,Vaibhav, asked when there was no Universe in existence where was the Creator standing? The readers of Ṛig-Veda can reply to these questions.

The ancient observers were of pure mind and were very close to the various truths of the Universe. Hence, the knowledge and observations presented by them in the form of the books of Veda need to be understood, not just worshipped.

Radhika Raman Prasad Sinha

February 26, 2008

गुरुर् ब्रह्मा, गुरूर् विष्णुर्; गुरूर् देवो महेश्वरः !
गुरूः साक्षात् परब्रह्मा; तस्मै श्रीगुरवे नमः !!

Gurur Brahma Gurur Vishnu Gurur Devo Maheshwaraha l
Guru Saakshat Para Brahma Tasmai Shree Gurave Namaha ll

Meaning:

Guru represents Brahma,Vishnu and Shiva. He creates, sustains knowledge and destroys ignorance. I salute such a Guru.

Preface

The Ṛig-Veda is a treasure of scientific observations made by ancient scholars (hereafter referred to as Rishis). The Rishis were Drashtas (Seers).

The observations were recorded in a form that would not slip into obscurity. The Rishis also had an additional challenge—to describe infinite knowledge in finite words. For example, the Sanskrit word "gau" means cow, in general. However, a scholar can interpret the word "gau" in more than forty ways and decode its meaning differently in the context of different verses. Similarly, there are many words such as horse, snake, bull, lamb, goat etc. each with several possible interpretations.

Secondly, the Rishis with pure heart observed and personified elements of nature and its fundamental laws. In one of the verses of Ṛig-Veda "Indra" is described as the Rain-God. Lightning is said to be Indra's weapon. In another verse the word Indra means the Sun. To understand these observations the meaning of Indra has to be decoded. The modern science has proved that the Sun controls all the planets by gravitational force. Also, raindrops fall to the earth as they are pulled by gravity. It is quite possible that Indra is a personification of gravitational force according to Rishis.

The Rishis in their state of super-consciousness heard the nature whispering her secrets and presented it in poetry with seemingly simple words, but very deep in meaning. The Rishis sang with rules of music not as yet copied by any musician. The Rishis' thoughts are Mantras and are known as Reecha, Riks, or hymns.

In the book of Ṛig-Veda there are lots of symbolism, parallelism, mysticism, and imagery. Scholars of literature can properly understand. One has to search for the cues in order to understand the hymns after decoding.

The first book of Veda is Ṛig-Veda. From this Veda has come the three Vedas, Yajur-Veda, Sam-Veda and Atharwa-Veda. These four books are associated with the fundamental truths required for good living. The first requirement is knowledge and Ṛig-Veda is for the knowledge. The second requirement is action and labor. Without efforts, survival cannot be possible. Yajur means action and so the second is Yajur-Veda. Another requirement is assimilation, accumulation and utilization of the earnings from work. This is a Atharwa-Veda. And, finally, relaxation and peace at the end of life. So, Sam-Veda is relevant to dance and music.

Every book of Veda is divided into three parts. mandala, sukta, rik or hymn. Mandalas are a congregation of suktas and suktas are congregation of hymns (also known as riks, mantras or reechas). So to locate any hymn or Rik, the three ordinates are wanted - mandala, sukta, rik (A.B.C). In this book, dealing with Ṛig-Veda, A B C are pertaining to the Ṛig-Veda only. If all the four books of Veda are in consideration, then the Veda also has to be mentioned. For example I (A B C) means Ṛig-Veda (A B C). II (A B C) means Yajur-Veda (A B C), III means Atharwa Veda and IV means Sam-Veda.

A rik or hymn may be cited as 1.113.10 which means first mandala, 113 sukta, 10th rik (hymn). Here one example is being highlighted. This is the tenth hymn of the Sukta 113 of the first mandala of Ṛig-Veda. This Hymn is in praise of dawn, personified as a beautiful lady—Usha.

Usha (dawn) is considered a Goddess, daughter of the Sun and sister of Ratri (night). She has unparalleled beauty and benevolent nature. She brings light before arrival of the Sun and together with her sister Ratri moves ceaselessly.

kiyātyā yat samayā bhavāti yā vyūṣuryāśca nūnaṃvyuchān |

anu pūrvāḥ kṛpate vāvaśānā pradīdhyānā joṣamanyābhireti ||

(1.113.10)

The translations of the above hymn about Usha by scholars like Wilson, Griffith, Muir, and Sharma are as follows:

Wilson: For how long a period is it that the dawns have arisen? For how long a period will they rise? Still desirous to bring us light, Usha pursues the function of those that have gone before and shining brightly precedes the others (that are to follow).

Griffith: How long a time they shall be together; dawns that have shone and dawns to shine hereafter? She yearns for former dawns with eager longing and goes forth gladly shining with the others.

Muir: How great is the interval that lies between the dawns, which have arisen and those which are yet to rise? Usha yearns longingly after the former dawns and gladly goes on shining with the others (that are to come).

Sharma: How long this Goddess Usha will remain here? Those who have arisen and those who will come in future, where will they remain for long duration? Recollecting the Ushas of the past, the present Usha is capable to illuminate. This Usha follows other Ushas.

The above translations suggest that "Usha follows the previous Ushas and precedes those that are to come."

This hymn can be understood with the help of astronomy and geography. The angle of incidence of the Sun's rays changes everyday. The earth's magnetic pole is not static. Some scientists believe that the elliptical path of the earth around the Sun also changes over time and that the Sun has movements of its own. All these subtle details about the Earth-Sun relations were known to the Rishis who sang the hymns about dawn, the Usha.

Millenniums before Newton, the Rishis sang the hymns indicating the seven colors (VIBGYOR) in radiant light as seven horses of the chariot of the Sun. They also sang verses indicating black holes millenniums before Einstein. In subsequent pages of this book many of such hymns containing scientific concepts will be cited.

It is given that the modern-day science is yet to make an instrument fine enough to record the observations made by the ancients. It is also a challenge to describe the treasures of Vedas in the language of the modern secular world with all its human limitations. At the same time it must be understood that the state of spiritual or mental elevation that was attained by the ancients is within the reach of the men and women of today and future. Quoting Swami Vivekananda "India had hundreds of Rishis in the past; India will have millions of Rishis in future." He also said—"book-worship is the worst form of idolatry."

The Vedas must be read and must also be understood. Swami Dayanand Saraswati, a great Vedic scholar, reformer, and awakener of Hindus against blind idolatry, indicated science and technology in the Vedas. Another great Indian—Lokmanya Balgangadhar Tilak, a scholar, reformer and freedom fighter, interpreted Veda with a scientific mind and presented his views in his books— "Arctic Home in the Vedas" and "Orion."

Sri Aurbindo has eulogized the works of Dayanand Saraswati and Balgangadhar Tilak in his book—"The Secrets of Veda." Among scolars of the west, T.H. Griffith has presented an elaborate translation of the hymns of Ṛig-Veda. Besides Griffith, other Vedic scholars from the west are Wilson, Muir, and Max Muller.

With advancement of science and technology scholars and scientists have more insight now; therefore, decoding and interpretation of Vedic hymns should be easier. In the absence of scientific background, the hymns cannot be decoded and remain almost unintelligible.

Vedic hymns have at least five dimensions: literature, spiritualism, science, music and effects of music on animate and inanimate objects. Therefore, as indicated by Max Muller, it is beyond the capability of a single scholar to unravel the truths of Ṛig-Vedic hymns. What is needed is a faculty of scholars representing different specializations.

With due respect to the aforesaid authors whose works have been quoted at several places, this book is a humble attempt to decode and interpret the scientific observations hidden in the hymns of Ṛig-Veda. These hymns contain deep truths of science, which can be understood and explained by a group of scholars.

The inspiration for this book came from my spiritual Guru, from the elders in my family, and from my younger brother, late Prof. B.B.Lal, a scholar of Botany.

There are some repetitions in this book. They are for emphasizing points which are normally misunderstood or are not generally known. Successful would be this book, if it inspires students and scholars of Science.

Let the Almighty bless all.

"The language of the Veda itself is sruti, a rhythm not composed by the intellect but heard, a divine Word that same vibrating out of the Infinite to the inner audience of the man who had previously made himself fit for the impersonal knowledge."

– Sri Aurobindo

What is Veda

The word "Ved" or "Veda" is a word of Sanskrit. The root of the word Veda is Sanskrit "Vid" meaning "for knowledge"; therefore, Veda means knowledge of truth.

Veda is as old as the earth or even older because the truths of nature existed before this earth and Sun came into existence. From western point of view, Vedas are only a few thousand years old. However, it is not essential to go into this debate. There is no controversy on the fact that the books of Veda are full of knowledge.

Knowledge can be classified as spiritual or material knowledge. The material is known as science. The material knowledge is gained by using the senses of the human body and reasoning. The spiritual knowledge is gained in deep meditation. But the knowledge gained in the state of super-consciousness is Veda which is total knowledge encompassing spiritual and material. The super-conscious state can be understood by knowing the stages of consciousness.

Most of us are aware of the first three stages of consciousness —awake, sleep, and dreaming; but, are unaware of the remaining stages which are higher than these three. The fourth stage is called Turiya. It is the stage between the stage of awake and the stage of sleep. Everybody goes through Turiya stage every day, but does not understand. The fifth stage is Bhagwat and the sixth is Ati Bhagwat. The last stage, seventh, is Brahmi.

The fourth stage—Turiya, is the place of Lord Shiva the personified power, Rudra of nature and also the Atma which is a part of the infinite power, the "Absolute". Because of the proximity between Shiva and Atma, Shiva represents Atma which is infinite. This fourth stage of timelessness gives immense pleasure. Yogis remain in this stage for long hours. So one can understand why yogis do not attach importance to worldly pleasures. In meditation, it is not very difficult to reach the fourth stage. What is needed is determination and practice, says Shankaracharya, who is said to be incarnation of Lord Shiva and who revived Sanatan Dharma. He has advised to practice meditation in his book—Vivekacudamani.

Yogis always try to reach the seventh stage—Brahmi. A few in millennium such as Buddha, Christ, and Mohammed, reach the seventh stage. They attained such knowledge which remained beyond time and space. They spoke the same truth, albeit, with different words. The Rishis who spoke the hymns of the Veda were persons of super-consciousness which is the Brahmi stage, perhaps.

The Veda is impersonal and contains truths which are above time and space. The hymns address different topics—spiritual, social, and scientific.

Rishis of the Vedic period were not interested in this gross body that we know, but in another body—the subtle body.

> "The subtle body is made out of the five organs of action and five organs of knowledge, the group of five pranas together with mind and desires. This subtle body or linga body, is produced out of the nascent elements, is possessed of latent impressions and causes the soul to experience the fruits of its past actions."—Vivekacudamani.

Both these bodies are always together. Rishis were associated with their subtle bodies. The vision and intellect of this gross body is limited and bound by time and space. But the field of the subtle body is infinite. This has been explained in Vivekacudamani referred to earlier.

This concept of limitation (gross body) and infiniteness (subtle body) belonged to two groups of Aryans. One of these groups settled in Greece and the other settled in the area now called India. The Greeks started observing the external field with the help of the gross body while the Indians were observing the inner field with their subtle bodies. The observations of the Greek Aryans moved towards west Europe and later to America and the observations of the Indian Aryans moved towards the East.

The observation of this gross body gave science, technology, and material pleasures. The observation of the subtle body gave rise to discussions, realizations, persuasion, and the view of inner self. The Indians, though strong with knowledge of science and technology, as would be evident in the hymns of Ṛig-Veda Samhita, disliked savagery and war as the Rishis had realized their inner-self through meditation.

However, the Indians did fight war whenever righteousness was subdued by evils. This led to wars between Ram and Ravana in which arms and strategies, many of which still not manufactured, were used. There is mention of supersonic air crafts and ground-to-air missiles capable of bringing down planes without harming the craft or its pilot. As mentioned in epic Mahabharata, there were weapons that artifially created tornadoes and covered the sky with dark clouds. In the field of medicine, as well, significant advancements were made during the period of Rama. There were medicines to cure punctured wounds instantaneously, to remove cut marks immediately, and to bring a fainted person back to consciousness within seconds.

And from where did all such science and technology come? These are offshoots of knowledge and knowledge of all topics is in the Vedas. This will be elucidated in the coming chapters. Rishis of the Vedic period were making such observations with pure heart and mind in the state of super-consciousness and presented their findings in poetry with beautiful words.

There were Rishis and some elevated more than Rishis were Maharishis like Narada, whose intelligence lay in speaking truth at opportune and right moment and as a result he initiated many changes for the good of people in general. Modern journalists should note this.

The Rishis were ordinary living persons like us. In the state of super-consciousness they could hear the whispers of Atma and Nature, collected knowledge from the whispered words and made efforts by meditation to realize those truths.

Knowing and realizing are poles apart. Here a few words may be added to elucidate the difference between knowledge and realization. Many of us know that God or Nature is controlling all activities outside and inside of our bodies. But how many believe in this knowledge or realize it? One may take an example of kidney or heart. If kidney, a small organ of body fails, a large dialysis machine is required to do the work of kidney. One can think of open heart surgery and the heart and lung machine. What does it take to design a pump like heart, on average 300 grams in weight, working at about 30 volts continuously?

An average human body is equivalent to about 45 watts. With such little power, energy and expenditure, Almighty is working through nature. We all must have this realization. Those who realize His greatness become great Rishis like Buddha, Christ, and Mohammed. Buddha realized Him through knowledge, Christ realized Him through love, and Mohammed realized Him through actions. So, these three are respectively Gyan yogi, Bhakta, and Karma yogi. Their greatness lies in realization of the Absolute.

Common people may worship His greatness but not all may realize it. Once this realization settles among masses, there would be no hatred, no deceit, no wars between people of different faiths and religions. All will see Him in every human body, plant, animal, in all animate and inanimate objects and hence nobody will like to harm, humiliate or ignore others. There would be peace all around. And this is the core teaching of "Vedanta" which means the end of Vedas.

Rishis had realization. They did reasoning as well. They framed hymns so that the progeny may know the eternal truths of nature and the wishes of the Absolute functioning through nature. The hymns, which are called Richas or Mantra or Riks, realized eternal truths. Rishis are called "Mantra drashta", which means seers of eternal truth.

The Rishis also hinted as to who can understand the meaning of the hymns. One Rishi said that the words of the hymn are in "Param Vyom" where all Gods reside and the right person can understand the meaning of the verses. Param Vyom is a Vedic word. The commonly understood meaning is "the highest heaven." A person with pure heart and mind and strong desire to know Him can reach the Param Vyom through meditation. Another Rishi says that for those who are "awake" the hymns are longing for them because "knowledge seeks the seeker". Here the meaning of "awake" is a state of high intellect gained through meditation.

Another Rishi has figuratively said that the hymns of Veda are like "a very beautiful dressed-up women" who undresses herself only for her husband. The husband is obviously a person with pure mind and heart and has attained super consciousness through meditation. Her beautiful dress represents the words of a hymn, and her beautiful body is the meaning of the hymn.

Rishis were large-hearted and hinted at the manner in which the meaning of the hymns can be understood. They did not conceal anything. For ordinary persons the Rishis gave music to sing the hymns. As stated earlier, the fourth Veda known as Sam-Veda, the origin of which is the Ṛig-Veda, is full of dance and music.

A Rishi is one of the three parts of a book of Veda, the other two being Devta and Chhanda. When the three, Rishi-Devta-Chhanda merge together, it is called Samhita which indicates assimilation. A book of Veda is a Samhita like the Ṛig-Ved Samhita. There is an interpretation that at the time of opening the book of Veda, with desire to read, the first message is "one diversified into many and many assimilated into one". On a higher plane, this means that one Absolute is in many forms and all forms join into one Absolute.

Devta and Chhanda, are worth knowing. Devta means the God, the subject on which Rishis have framed the hymns. The Chhanda is the metre, which is suitable to convey the meaning of the subject. Some define the combination of Rishi-Devta-Chhanda in Sanskrit as Gyata-Gyan-Gyeya, which means the observer, the matter observed and the process of observation.

The Ṛig-Veda and the other three Vedas, Yajur-Veda, Atharwa-Veda, and Sam-Veda which are born out of Ṛig-Veda are musically oriented with different Chhandas. The Chhandas can be explained as the different *ragas* of the Indian music. The most common Chhanda is Gayatri and the most common and revered verse is: "Om bhurbhuwa Swah, tat saviturvareṇyaṃ bhargho devasya dhīmahi | dhiyo yo naḥ pracodayāt ||" This is dedicated to the rising Sun, also called Savita, and means "may the Almighty God illuminate our mind to lead us to the righteous path."

Ṛig-Veda has ten mandalas. Seven of the ten mandalas have a Rishi of special importance. The first mandala is general. The second mandala has the importance of Rishi Gritsmada, the third associated with Vishwamitra, the fourth with Vamdeo, the fifth with Atri, the sixth with Bharadwaj, the seventh with Vashistha, the eighth and tenth are general like the first mandala. The ninth mandala is especially for Som—generally interpreted as divine wine but actually it is cosmic frequency or energy. The entire Veda is melodious and gives bliss (Ananda) to the singer and listener of hymns.

From Vedas came Brahmans, the book for Yagya, and social laws. Also from Vedas came Upnishads. The Brahman books were written by Brahmins (priests). Later on from Brahman developed priesthood. So Brahmans are sometimes called Karmkand meaning chapters for duties and Yagyas.

The Hindus consider Veda as *Apaurushava* which means "not belonging to a person". They consider hymns of the Vedas as the words spoken by Him. The Rishis listened to His words and presented to the masses in a form that can be memorized and sung. That is why Veda is called Shruti meaning "heard", and all other subsequent literatures, written with Vedas as the root, are called Smritis for example, the Puranas. The Shruti is to be accepted when differing with Smriti at any point. The Smritis are inferior to Shrutis.

From time immemorial the musicians of India follow the guidelines of metres, rhythm etc, given in Ṛig-Veda and later in Sam-Veda. As music has no barriers of nationality, caste, religion, or race, music is said to be *Karnamitria* (nectar through ears).

It is singing of hymns from generations to generations that the Vedas are alive, albeit not as a whole. Many hymns are said to be lost with the families who did not propagate. It is said that the last Veda, Sam-Veda had hundred and above branches, but all are lost except for the few verses available now-a-days.

It was the great intellectual sage Ved Vyasa who collected all the available hymns and compiled the Ṛig-Veda and the other three Vedas—Yajur-Veda, Atharwa-Veda, and Sam-Veda. It is believed that the contributions of Ved Vyasa have been fully preserved and there has not been any loss of hymns after him.

Here one point is to be noted. The Rishis in Veda were called singers. Their hymns of eternal truth were for singing and not for speech or lecture. To convey the truth they used wonderful similes, the elements of nature, and animals. As stated earlier, for singing they formulated many metres called Chhanda. There is an exhaustive book, called Shastra on Chhanda. These Chhandas are the basis of modern Ragas. The Rishis had a level of perfection in singing which the modern singers are yet to reach. For example, at present there are three known Laya (pause) in music, namely—slow, normal and fast. The Rishis are said to know seven Laya. Perhaps, the Rishis constant nearness to Him- the infinite, transpired into infinite range of music as well.

The following chapters will explore the concepts of nature and various Gods and Goddesses who have been represented in the hymns of Ṛig-Veda. It must be noted that the Gods and Goddesses are personifications of the forces of nature such as—gravitation, motion, mass and energy, astronomical events and geological processes.

Nature

Commonly speaking, Nature is associated with stars, planets, animate and inanimate objects, life and death, behavior, and character. The Chamber's Dictionary defines Nature as "the physical world not made by man, the forces that have formed it and control it."

For philosophers and students of the book of Veda, Nature means "differentiation" as this nature makes one Absolute into finite units. The Absolute is He the Supreme and under Him the nature has her realm.

The Supreme is the father and Nature is the mother, as such, Nature gives birth to infinite aspects of the Universe. In this creation or say the realm of Nature, there are seemingly many contradictions and the contradictions may be due to ignorance. The laws or behavior of Nature are very simple but for ignorant these may appear complicated. A question arises as to why the Supreme He is considered Father. The reason can be explained by a simple experiment.

Medical science knows the quantities of elements—calcium, iron, carbon present in a normal human body. Can the same be used to create a human form artificially? What is that which transforms the combination of gross items, the elements, into a lively and intelligent being? The answer is He.

Philosophers say the five elements—earth, water, fire, sky, and air (in Sanskrit: Kshiti, Jal, Pawak, Gagan, Samira) were combined to create life. One can see that these are arranged from gross to subtle. Earth (solid), water (liquid), fire (visible vibration), sky (the infinite space), and lastly, air (the invisible vibration). The scientific aspects have been simplified for ease of comprehension. These five also give life only when He acts.

Except in case with identical twins a mother does not give birth to two children of exactly the same face, or behavior. All born of the same mother have different behaviors, and different ways of life. So there is differentiation. In Sanskrit Nature means *Prakriti* meaning differentiation.

The Rishis saw similarities within these differentiations. They saw unity amidst diversity, simplicity amidst complexities, and the sanctity of various laws of Nature which are never broken or modified.

The modern Rishis, scientists like Newton, and Einstein, were above ordinary human beings so they could observe the nature and understand some of the eternal truths. What they observed about laws of gravitation, motion, mass and energy, have existed since time immemorial.

Similar were the Rishis who heard and saw the Nature's activities and presented their findings in hymns to be sung by everyone and its deeper meanings to be understood by elevated minds. They saw Nature as the representative of the Absolute. The Rishis very boldly said "Neti, Neti, Neti," meaning what they know was not the end. Thus acknowledging that their knowledge was not the ultimate. *Neti* is a Sanskrit word consisting of two words; Na (means no) and Etee (means end). Hence, *Neti* means not the end of knowledge.

Rishi

Rishis were observers of the eternal truths. The Rishis who spoke the hymns of the Veda were persons of super-consciousness. They could hear the Absolute whispering its laws and transmitted those laws to the humanity, not in prose but in poems to be sung.

Externally, the Rishis were like any other human, but internally they were always in search of eternal truth. Rishis had wives, and children. Children were born after prayer and desire for a good child.

Rishis had pure self and pure intellect which is called "Atmashuddhi" and "Chittashuddhi". They could hear the whispers of Atma and Nature, collect knowledge from the whispered words and realize the knowledge through meditation.

The Rishis were above caste and gender. Persons of all Verna (social hierarchy) were Rishis. Women were also Rishis. To attain Rishihood the cleansing of self and intellect, (Atmashuddhi and Chittashuddhi) was needed and not affiliation to a particular social order.

For common persons, the Rishis were praising the Absolute through sweet musical songs (hymns) but for persons of high intellect interested in knowing higher truths, the Rishis were telling the secrets of Him and Nature.

The Rishis were completely devoted to Him, the Absolute, and sublimated themselves into Him. For the Rishis, only He and His laws existed and nothing else. Rishis did not give much information about themselves, their place of birth, their parentage, or the period or time of their hymns. Efforts are being made to know the personal details of the Rishis. Henry Thomas Colebrooke, an officer of the East India Company, a Sanskrit scholar and President of the Asiatic Society who made significant contributions towards preservation of Indian heritage, has calculated the Vedic calendar to be 1400 BCE approximately. This reflected on further antiquity of hymns. However, this estimate is controversial.

Like an ordinary person, Rishis were vulnerable to strong tentacles of desires for sensuous pleasures. Sometimes, such desires overpowered them. Here is the story of Maharishi Vishwamitra as an example.

> Once Maharishi Vishwamitra fell in love with a court dancer named Menaka, and fathered a beautiful girl named, Shakuntala. However, they abandoned her upon birth, obviously a cruel and mean act. This child of Vishwamitra and Menaka was brought up by Rishi Kanva. As the story goes, a king fell in love with Shakuntala and before their marriage Shakuntala's son Bharat was born. This baby Bharat spent his childhood under love and guidance of Rishi Kanva (who had also brought up Shakuntala). Bharat grew up to be a very powerful monarch. The region he ruled was also known as Bharat which eventually became the country of India. Of course with historical upheavals changes came in the geographical area of Bharat.

This story has a deeper message over and above the external meanings like sensuous pleasure, love at first sight, child born before marriage, and lust of kings. This story refers to the extent of knowledge the Rishis had in order to raise a child who would eventually rule a powerful kingdom. The Rishis not only had spiritual knowledge, as is normally known, but also practical skills such as knowledge of weapons, and wars. This message is in epic Ramayana also as follows:

> Rishi Balmiki reared the two sons Luv and Kush of exiled Sita, wife of Lord Rama. The Rishi trained Luv and Kush and made them so powerful that these two young boys defeated great warriors like Mahabir and their uncle Lakshman and even Rama had to surrender albeit tactfully showing love of a father for sons.

Such were the power and knowledge of the Rishis. But these Rishis themselves preferred to live far away from the masses.

The story of Maharishi Vishwamitra and Menaka has another aspect too—the power of Maya over Rishis. What is Maya? In Sanskrit Ma means 'no' and Ya means 'which'. Thus Maya means something that does not exist but appears as if real. It may be said that Maya is illusion similar to mirage in a desert. It is Maya that overwhelmed Vishwamitra as a result he was involved with a court dancer Menaka.

Maya is personified as a beautiful damsel, very enchanting, intelligent and opportunist, befooling all and loving none. Knowledge is personified as male and Bhakti (devotion) towards God as a female. Maya invariably overpowers knowledge but never a Bhakta (devotee) of God. So Rishis were vulnerable. Here is an allegory given by Saint Ramakrishna: "a cat lifts her baby (kitten) by teeth and the kitten remains unharmed, but a mouse held like that dies. Maya does not destroy a Bhakta."

A student of science can understand Maya. If an object is rotating around a center, two forces are acting on the object. These are the centripetal and centrifugal forces. If humans are considered as revolving around the center which is the Absolute (Parmatma), then the centripetal force is knowledge and centrifugal force is Maya which overpowered even Rishis and Maharishis. Maya is associated with pleasure of senses belonging to the external world and is non-permanent. The Indriyas or senses are tools of Maya. Control over Indriya is the goal of Rishis for achieving internal clarity and for observing eternal truths.

Rishis have many categories, commonly known as: Maharishi, Rajrishi, Brahmarishi, and Devrishi. The Aryans of the Vedic period believed in the infinite strength of every human being and everyone's capacity to attain Rishihood.

The names of several Rishis have come to prominence. Seven of them are so much glorified that the seven visible stars of the constellation, the Saptarishi, commonly known as the Great Bear or Ursa Major are named after seven Maharishis. They are—Marici, Atri, Angiras, Pulastya, Pulaha, Kratu, and Vasistha, who will be introduced hereafter.

Marici: The word Marici means "ray of light" or a "grain of light". A student of science may like to decipher as to what is meant by a "grain of light". Marici was a Brahma's son.

Atri: One meaning of Atri is traveler. He was thrown by demons in a fire pit. Indra saved him. He is also favoured by the twin Gods Aswins. He rescued Sun when eclipsed. It is Indra who showed him hundred ways of escape from captivity. Atri does not appear to be any person. It is some force of energy existing in Nature in various forms. Atri also means eater or Agni. He is said to be one of the ten sons of Brahma and born out of Brahma's eyes.

Angiras: Among all, Angiras has much prominence in Veda. He is considered semi divine and belonging to a race of higher beings between Gods and men. Angiras formulated rituals to be followed by others. The descendents of Angiras dwell in the solar sphere. There are enough hints to identify Angiras with solar rays.

Pulastya: He is well-known as the maternal grand father of Ravana, the emperor who was defeated by Rama. Rishi Pulastya was Manasputra of Brahma. Manasputra is a Sanskrit word coined of Manas meaning thought or desire and Putra meaning son.

Pulaha: It is said that Rishi Pulaha was the Manasputra (a son born of thought) of Brahma. Thought also means force as explained by Swami Vivekananda. Pulaha must be a type of force emanating from Brahma. According to Vedic literature, force comes out of knowledge. Brahma means infinite knowledge. So, Pulaha is some type of force in the Universe.

Kratu: He was one among the ten sons of Brahma. The word Kratu means knowledge, intellect, strength, ability. Quoting Wilson and Griffith (both being translators of Veda in English) Kratu means Karma (act) or Prajna (knowledge).

Vashistha: He was for social laws and politics. Vashistha remained closer to Kings.

In Ṛig-Veda, other Rishis have been mentioned. These are Bharadwaj, Kashyap, Gautama, Vishwamitra, Yamadagni, and Bhargava.

Among the above Rishis, Maharishi Vishwamitra was mostly science-oriented and less inclined to spiritualism. The descendents of Vishwamitra, like other Rishis, continued with their surname in the period of Lord Rama also. Rockets, satellites were creation of Vishwamitra. Tuber crops such as potato, onion were also developed by Vishwamitra. In Sanskrit, Vishwamitra means "friend of the Universe".

In Hindu religious books there are many examples of rise of fallen men or women to Rishihood. There are examples of robbers, butchers, or prostitutes who attained the real pleasure called bliss which is internal pleasure, after submissions and realization of Him—the Infinite.

The Rishis say that He does not break His laws. He has made the laws of nature and He lives inside those laws, like the Sun who creates clouds and keeps himself hidden behind the cloud. This simile is applied to Atma, who is His faction inside everybody.

As a fraction of infinite is infinite, so Atma as a part of Him, the infinite, is also infinite existing in microcosm as well as macrocosm. The Rishis were devoted to realization of the infinity. The Rishis had full understanding of the smaller than the smallest and the larger than the largest. He the Infinite, exists everywhere, the Rishis had realized. This fundamental truth is also in the song celestial Gita.

Perhaps the sages have used the color blue to visualize or realize infinity. If one stands on the seashore, one sees only blue up to a very long distance. Similarly, if one looks towards the sky one sees blue color to an unimaginable distance. Is this the reason that Lord Rama and Lord Krishna are said to be of blue complexion? Is it because they are considered as incarnation of Him, the Infinity?

One can read innumerable books concerning Rama or Krishna but very few can realize the expanse of their greatness and wisdom. Gita, the song celestial, given by Lord Krishna is still not fully understood and realized. Sages and philosophers and intellectual giants have spent their life in understanding and explaining Gita which has its root in Vedic hymns, sung by Rishis. One can imagine the expanse of the intellect and greatness of Rishis. None can fathom their depth of love and wisdom. It was love in their hearts that led Rishis to a pure life externally as well as internally in order to realize Him for the sake of progeny to whom the Rishis gave eternal truths in the form of hymns to sing.

"Every force completes a circuit. The force we call man starts from the Infinite God and must return to Him."

– Swami Vivekananda

The Gods and Goddesses

There are 33 Gods and Goddesses in the Ṛig-Veda. The Rishis have presented the various forces, energies, space, and vibrations as Gods. The order in which Gods are placed is very meaningful.

Gods can be formless or with forms and all Gods are but different creations or projections of the Paramatma or the Ultimate, Supreme, Omnipotent, and Omnipresent. This unity amidst diversity is the core preaching of the Rishis.

The first God is He, the Ultimate Supreme, the Infinite. Next, there is the Triad known as the Holy Trinity. They are Brahmaspati, Vishnu, and Rudras (Tryambaka), commonly known as Brahma, Vishnu, and Mahesh (Shiva). In their formless representation Brahma is thought, Vishnu is space and Rudra is the force uplifting thoughts. Later on, these three have been understood as infinite knowledge, infinite space for action and Mahesh (Shiva) as the infinite force, initially, but later as the infinite peace and tranquility. Among these three, Shiva has the maximum number of worshippers. Shiva is the highest God (Mahadev). He is also called Mahakal—the great time where there is only present, no past or future. Shiva is Rudra at rest, when Shiva danced as Rudra, the dance is known as Tandav dance. When in peace Shiva danced with his wife Parvati and the dance is known as Lasya dance. While Tandav dance is horrifying, Lasya dance is very sensuous. When in peace, Shiva gave five Ragas (melodic forms) out of the total six Ragas of music. His wife gave the sixth, Raga Malkosh. When at rest, Parvati sits on the left thigh of Shiva. They have three sons Ganesh – the youngest, Kartikeya – the eldest, and Skanda – the middle one who is not commonly known.

In pictures Shiva is shown as motionless, in meditation, with slightly open eyelids and snakes, scorpions crawling over his motionless body.

In pictures Vishnu is shown as sleeping on the coil of a large snake floating in an ocean of milk.

Brahma is shown to have four heads, four hands each holding one Veda, and sitting on a lotus the root of which is in the naval of Vishnu sleeping on the coil of the snake mentioned above.

For proper understandings, Gods have to be de-personified. The example of Shiva, Parvati, and their sons – Kartikeya, Skanda and Ganesh may be taken. Shiva means mass at rest (tranquility). Intense tranquility often precedes intense activity such as storm, volcanic eruption, and submarine earthquake that generates giant waves or tsunamis. The energy of all these intense activity is Parvati. In simple words, Shiva is the matter and Parvati is the energy. Consequent to this conversion of matter into energy, the radiation of ultraviolet (UV) zone is known as Ganesh, of infrared (IR) zone is Kartikeya, and the middle zone is Skanda. The zone of UV rays is not very large, but maximum energy is in UV rays. It is said that Ganesh does not travel very far from his parents and Ganesh is the most powerful and has the first oblation in any worship.

Kartikeya means IR rays which travels large distances. Skanda is the middle zone of radiation and important for living beings. That is why among the eighteen Puranas, the Skanda Purana is the most voluminous as it deals with practically all aspects of life.

The concept of Shiva, Parvati and their sons can be best understood by scholars of Physics who can interpret mass-energy conversion. Analysis of UV rays can explain why Ganesh is represented with a large body and his carrier is a mouse.

In the absence of a sound understanding of the scientific theories one could not comprehend such complexities. Therefore, many higher truths spoken by Rishis have been misconstrued. The ancients gave personifications such as Shiva, and Vishnu. God Vishnu is shown as sleeping on a snake (python) with many hoods, floating in an ocean of milk. Mostly, people worship this image of Vishnu without understanding that the snake, known as Anant, literally means without end (infinite); the coils represent the cycles of creation and annihilations. After annihilation called, Pralaya in Sanskrit, the space (Vishnu) becomes motionless meaning He sleeps. The ocean denotes infinity in which the cycles of creation and annihilation are taking place. Students of Physics can understand the triodes as M(Mass), L(Length), and T(Time), where Mass is Brahma, Length is Vishnu, and Time is Shiva and all these three are always together in energy, force, power, or work.

After the Triads—Brahma, Vishnu, Rudra (Shiva or Mahesh) are many Gods and Goddesses of prime importance and then of lesser importance.

Aditi

The first is Aditi, a Goddess, mother of all Gods. Her father is Daksha Prajapati and she is wife of Kashyap. She is also considered as mother of the Adityas (Sun). She is mother of God Indra also. When de-personified, she is considered as pure consciousness of infinite existence, self luminous, free, secure, and sinless. Aditi is the expanse of infinite dimension encompassing all Gods and matter.

The most powerful son of Aditi is Indra. When Indra was born Aditi gave him Som prior to breast feeding. Indra means all types of forces personified. The most important force is gravitation and Indra generally means gravitational force. Similarly, Som is not a drink but cosmic waves or frequency.

Now, when Aditi is endless infinite expense then what is the real identity of Daksha and Kashyap, her father and husband respectively? Daksha is creative power. Kashyap is the name of a Rishi who is son of Rishi Marici. Rishi Marici is son of Brahma.

There is another puzzling point concerning Aditi. Scientists may decode, analyze, and decipher for the truth. The point is that Aditi gave birth to Daksha and was subsequently born as daughter of Daksha. This suggests that the infinite consciousness and creative power are related.

The relationship has been reflected in the Aryan theory of Creation of the Universe. According to Aryan theory, there is no creation or destruction. The Aryans believed in the change of form which is similar to the principle of conservation of energy. After the establishment of relation between matter and energy ($E=MC^2$) the realm of this conservation of energy has become as large as infinity. With this concept the Aryans believed in two things—Aakash (Ether) and Pran (Force). Aakash is space comprising matter in infinitely minute forms. Pran is the force which vibrates Aakash and creates galaxies, stars, planets, and life. This vibration continues for certain period and then stops and the entire projection is converted into Aakash.

If we look into this concept of creation then the Aakash is Aditi and the force Pran is Daksha and projections, creations are taking place according to various laws and energy or forces, known as Gods for example, heat energy (God Agni), and gravitational force (God Indra). If it is further analyzed then concepts of the Triad becomes clear. The space is Vishnu, the force is Rudra (Shiva) and the laws, as a whole, are represented by Brahma.

This concept of projection and destruction is in song celestial —Gita, wherein Krishna says that there is nothing like birth or death. It is like changing of dress for the infinite (atma) which resides in the gross body of humans as well as every living being plants, and animals. This may be interpreted by the scholars of science as conservation of energy and also as conservation of matter.

Agni

The next important God is Agni. He is said to be the son of Brahma. Agni is all types of energy personified. The Rishis recognized superiority of energy over force. So they held Agni superior to Indra. That is why the Ṛig-Veda starts with Rik of Agni -

aghnimīḷe purohitaṃ yajñasya devaṃ ṛtvījam |
hotāraṃ ratnadhātamam || (1.1.1)

This hymn praises Agni as Purohit, priest, inviter of Gods and giver of wealth. Purohit means a priest who foresees the proper interest of his followers. Agni is Ritwik (chief priest) of Gods and in this capacity, He performs Yagyas; Agni is "hota", which means He invites Gods to come to the Yagya. Agni is also said to be a giver of gems. Yagya means work. For work, the first requisite (Purohit) is energy. As Gods are various forces they need energy. When energy is spent, forces arrive. All gems and minerals available below the earth surface, are formed by consuming the heat energy.

It is notable that the Rishi who had sung this Rik was Madhuchandas Vishwamitra. He is believed to be son of

Rishi Vishwamitra, from a Rajrishi family. Rajrishis are also known are vigyani (scientists having realization). This Rik is in the Chhanda Gayatri which is most prominent in Ṛig-Veda and most popular among Hindus.

In Sanskrit, the root word of Agni means "static" and also "not in linear movement". It is known that stored energy is static. When energy travels, it travels in waves. There may be a controversy if Newtonian view of propagation of light in linear manner is taken. But it is true that light travels in waves.

The Ṛig-Veda is full of Riks indicating various characteristics of energy. In fact, knowledge about energy is very vast. Ved Vyas has written Agni-Puran only to explain the importance of Agni. Agni can be understood by scholars of physics and chemistry. There are other points to prove that Agni is not just the fire as commonly known.

tvamaghne prathamo mātariśvana āvirbhava sukratūyā vivasvate |
arejetāṃ rodasī hotṛvūrye.asaghnorbhāramayajo mahovaso ||
(1.31.3)

When there was no Sun, the Agni existed. Here the Nebula is referred to. From Nebula came this entire solar system, according to one theory in Astronomy.

seneva sṛṣṭāmaṃ dadhātyasturna didyut tveṣapratīkā |
yamo ha jāto yamo janitvaṃ jāraḥ kanīnāṃ patirjanīnām ||
(1.66.70)

In this hymn, Griffith interprets Agni to be a lover of maidens. Agni is also husband of married women. Physicians and scholars of medical science can understand and explain this hymn. Normally, in human beings a maiden's behavior indicates her desire for offsprings. Perhaps, this energy is personified as Agni. As a corollary, one can say that for continuity of creation this energy expressed as Agni, is responsible.

abhi tvā ghotamā ghirā jātavedo vicarṣaṇe |
dyumnairabhi pra ṇonumaḥ || (1.78.1)

Agni knows and observes all of the secrets of creation.

trīṇi jānā pari bhūṣantyasya samudra ekaṃ divyekamapsu |
pūrvāmanu pra diśaṃ pārthivānāṃṛtūn praśāsadvi dadhāvanuṣṭhu ||
(1.95.3)

Agni originates at three places: in oceans, in sky and in Antariksha, a Sanskrit word which means "the space in between earth and Sun where water moisture does not exist." The most important observation of the Rishi had been existence of Agni in Ocean, a truth recently known to oceanographers who have discovered submarine volcanoes. In Sanskrit this fire is known as Barwanal. Such zones of heat have been discovered even underneath the icy continent of Antarctica.

Uta no.ahirbudhnyo mayas kaḥ śiśuṃ na pipyuṣīva veti sindhuḥ |
yena napātamapāṃ junāma manojuvo vṛṣaṇo yaṃ vahanti ||
(1.186.5)

The electricity in clouds is named Ahirbudhnya, a form of Agni. This form of Agni breaks the rain clouds so that rain may commence. The Rishis had known this much before Benjamin Franklin who explored the existence of electricity in clouds.

ā yasmin sapta raśmayastatā yajñasya netari |
manuṣvad daivyamaṣṭamaṃ potā viśvaṃ tadinvati || (2.5.2)

There are seven rays in Agni. According to Griffith, these seven are associated with seven priests. Science students can understand the seven rays of Agni. Perhaps it suggests the seven visible colors VIBGYOR.

The Rishis gave considerable importance to number seven. There are seven stages of consciousness in Yoga. It is possible that nature, if observed from seven different stages of consciousness, will give different results.

The Veda says that the Sun's chariot has seven horses. Influenced by this seven, the Rishis saw seven rivers of inspiration called Saraswati and similarly there are many truths associated with seven.

Agni is not destructible, it is benevolent and travels all around. Agni is associated with Jal which means fluid or water. Scientists may understand this word—Jal, as plasma.

According to Rishis the three fundamental forces are—Som, Jal, and Ap. According to Vedic science, combination of two of these three results into the third force. Perhaps, Som and Jal when combined gave gravitational force. The combination of Som and Ap gives electromagnetic force; and combination of Ap and Jal is nuclear force.

aibhiraghne sarathaṃ yāhyarvāṃ nānārathaṃ vā vibhavo hyaśvāḥ |
patnīvatastriṃśataṃ trīṃśca devānanuṣvadhamā vaha mādayasva ||
(3.6.9)

This hymn is a very scientific hymn. As per this hymn there are thirty-three Gods. Why thirty-three? The number thirty-three is also in 8.28.1, 8.30.2, 8.35.3. According to this hymn, Agni's chariot is capable of bringing all the thirty-three Gods together. The Rishi also prays to Agni to bring the Gods in different chariots if he likes. The Rishi also requests Agni to bring those Gods with their spouses to drink Som.

In Veda, chariot also represents wave. Spouse is synonym for complimentary forces. The number thirty-three represents eight Vasus, eleven Rudras, twelve Adityas, Prajapati and Vasilkara. The great Vedic scholar Wilson has accepted the above interpretation. Griffith has quoted Wilson's interpretation as above. The meaning of Vasus, Rudras, Adityas, Prajapati and Vasilkara will be stated in coming pages.

If one tries to understand nuclear particles, as per earlier research of Japanese physicist Hideki Yukawa and noble laureate physicist Richard P. Feynman, there are thirty-three particles. No theory exists whether these thirty-three are different aspects of the same thing. According to Rishi Vishwamitra and also by Rishis Hiranyastup Angiras, there are thirty-three fundamental Gods. Rishi Vishwamitra, however, indicates that these thirty-three Gods are connected with Agni. Physicists can evaluate Vishwamitra's views.

There is another interesting interpretation of thirty-three Gods. In Sanskrit it is said that there are thirty-three "Koti" Gods. In Sanskrit Koti means thirty-three as well as crore (a million). Due to this interpretation by some priests Hindus in general believe that there are thirty-three million Gods and this belief also leads to disunity among Hindus. The scientific interpretation leads to thirty-three Gods.

viśveṣām aditir yajñiyānāṃ viśveṣām atithir mānuṣāṇām |
aghnir devānām ava āvṛṇānaḥ sumṛḷīko bhavatu jātavedāḥ ||
(4.1.20)

This hymn is by Rishi Vamdeo who is as important for science scholars as Rishi Vishwamitra. In this hymn the Rishi says that Agni, like Aditi, gives birth to all Gods of Yagya (sacrifice). Agni accepts prayers of human beings and gives wealth, prosperity, and pleasure to the stotas (one who praises). It is to be noted that translation by Griffith is a little different. However, Rishi Vamdeo's views in this hymn are very much similar to the first hymn of Ṛig-Veda.

Rishi Vamdeo finds Agni (energy) as parent of all Gods of Yagya (action). It is again being emphasized upon that Yagya does not mean burning of wood, butter, or grains. Yagya means actions, dedicated actions for good cause. The Rishis also say that those who spend energy properly, get prosperity.

pāhi no aghna ekayā pāhyuta dvitīyayā |
pāhi ghīrbhistisṛbhirūrjāṃ pate pāhi catasṛbhirvaso || (8.60.9)

According to Griffith, Agni is son of strength. But the Hindi translation means Agni is master of all energies. Both are correct. The modern science has proved the production of heat by work done (transformation of mechanical or muscular energy into heat energy). The real meaning is Agni, personified as all types of energies.

sa tu vastrāṇyadha peśanāni vasāno aghnirnābhāpṛthivyāḥ |
aruṣo jātaḥ pada iḷāyāḥ purohito rājanyakṣīha devān || (10.1.6)

Agni's color at the center of this earth, as per this hymn, is as bright as gold. But as per Griffith the color is red. Definitely, this hymn refers to the color of magma, the fire at the center of this earth. It is for the Geologists to accept or reject this hymn. The entire mandala 10, sukta 5 is highly scientific and explains about energy. The first hymn (10.5.1) given below, identifies Agni as electricity in clouds.

ekaḥ samudro dharuṇo rayīṇāmasmad dhṛdo bhūrijanmā vicaṣṭe |
siṣaktyūdharniṇyorupastha utsasya madhyenihitaṃ padaṃ veḥ ||

In hymn 10.8.1 below Agni is electricity.

pra ketunā bṛhatā yātyaghnirā rodasī vṛṣabho roravīti |
divaścidantānupamānudānaḷ apāmupasthe mahiṣovavardha ||

The above discussion highlights only few of the many hymns devoted to Agni.

Indra

Indra is understood as the most powerful among Gods. Indra is all the forces personified. The Rishis have indicated repeatedly that Indra means force, especially gravitational force. Rishi Madhuchanda, with whose hymn commences Ṛig-Veda has introduced Indra jointly with Vayu in the second hymn of the first mandala. The Rishi indicates in sukta 3 hymn 6 that Indra is associated with horses.

indrā yāhi tūtujāna upa brahmāṇi harivaḥ |
sute dadhiṣvanaścanaḥ || (1.3.6)

In mandala 1 sukta 4 hymn 7, the Rishi describes Indra as a fast walker. In sukta 6 hymn 1 Indra's various forms are indicated. In the hymn 2 of the same sukta, there are two horses of Indra their color represented as that of blood. In sukta 7 hymn 2, Indra is presented as a unifier and organizer. The word unifier has to be noted. The above hymns are from the first mandala.

Considering that the Rishi of all these hymns is son of Vishwamitra, one has to think deeply to understand scientific truths in the above hymns. It would be great disrespect to the Rishi if the hymns are misconstrued to derive spiritual meanings. These hymns at the outset of Ṛig-Veda give the following scientific observations: a) movement of gravitation is very fast; b) gravitation exists in many forms; and c) gravitation is not linear but is a combination of two waves of red wavelength.

Rishi's theory has been partly upheld by modern wave concept of gravitational forces.

ā paprau pārthivaṃ rajo badbadhe rocanā divi |
na tvāvānindra kaścana na jāto na janiṣyate.ati viśvaṃ vavakṣitha ||
(1.81.5)

In hymn 1.8.5 above, Indra is said as a superintendent controlling authority of all constellations, earth and space above the earth. The concept of gravitation force, in the form of Indra, is very obvious.

yajñairatharvā prathamaḥ pathastate tataḥ sūryo vratapāvena ājani |
ā ghā ājaduśanā kāvyaḥ sacā yamasya jātamamṛtaṃ yajāmahe ||
(1.83.5)

This hymn indicates origin of the Sun, and subsequently earth and arrival of sun's rays to the earth, all these under the controlling authority of Indra.

sa sūnubhirna rudrebhirṛbhvā nṛṣāhye sāsahvānamitrān |
sanīḷebhiḥ śravasyāni tūrvan marutvno bhvatvindran uti || (1.100.5)

The above hymn indicates that Maruts help Indra. It needs to be further decoded to understand as to what assists gravitational force.

rohicchyāvā sumadaṃśurlalāmīrdyukṣā rāya ṛjrāśvasya |
vṛṣaṇvantaṃ bibhratī dhūrṣu rathaṃ mandrā ciketa nāhuṣīṣu vikṣu ||
(1.100.16)

This hymn indicates the color of the two horses of Indra's chariots. They are said to be Rohit (red) and Shyam (shining black or deep blue or deep green). But Griffith says red and tawny and he translates them to be mares and not horses.

takṣan rathaṃ suvṛtaṃ vidamnāpasastakṣan harī indravāhā vṛṣaṇvasū |
takṣan pitṛbhyāṃ ṛbhavo yuvad vayastakṣanvatsāya mātaraṃ sacābhuvam || (1.111.1)

Ribhu has trained Indra's horses. Regarding the number of horses there is unanimity, but regarding the color of horses there are different interpretations. In hymns 1.184.4 and 2.18.3 only two horses are mentioned but not their color.

The following three hymns are examined from mandala 2 sukta 18. (2.18.4, 2.18.5 and 2.18.6)

ā dvābhyāṃ haribhyāmindra yāhyā caturbhirā ṣaḍbhirhūyamānaḥ |
āṣṭābhirdaśabhiḥ somapeyamayaṃ sutaḥsumakha mā mṛdhas kaḥ ||
(2.18.4)

ā viṃśatyā triṃśatā yāhyarvāṃ ā catvāriṃśatā haribhiryajānaḥ |
ā pañcāśatā surathebhirindrā ṣaṣṭyā saptatyā somapeyam ||
(2.18.5)

āśītyā navatyā yāhyarvāṃ ā śatena haribhiruhyamānaḥ |
ayaṃ hi te śunahotreṣu soma indra tvāyā pariṣikto madāya ||
(2.18.6)

These are interesting hymns in which mathematical multiplication tables have been suggested. There is also reference to arithmetic progression from 2 to 4, 6, 8, 10, horses and also 20, 30, 40, 50, 60, 70, 80, 90, and 100 horses. It is anticipated that Indra's horses increase in number in the above manner. It has been established that Indra is gravitational force personified. Nowhere is it clarified as to why the Rishi gave such progressive numbers with reference to Indra (gravitational force). Scholars of Physics may think over it.

In hymn 3.30.6 Rishi Vishwamitra says the horses are of Harit varna (Sanskrit for green, yellow and yellow-green).

In mandala 3 hymns 40.1, 40.2, 40.8, and 43.6 and 44.2, the color of the two horses is indicated as Harit again. Griffith has translated it as bay and tawny. According to Chamber's dictionary "bay" means horses of reddish-brown color, normally with black mane and tail and tawny means reddish-brown.

In hymn 3 35.3 the color indicated in blood color, but Griffith translates it as tawny. Again, hymn 4.32.22 indicates color brown but Griffith translates it as tawny.

Hymn 7.21.1 suggests Harit (green, yellow, or yellow-green) horses. In hymn 8.93.24 the color of the horses mane is indicated as golden.

It appears to be a matter of research by scholars of Physics as to :

a) What is the nature of gravitational waves?

b) Are there two waves, parallel or helical like DNA?

c) To which spectrum do these waves belong?

One should not set aside the wave theory of Rishis about gravitation only because there is no unanimity on color. Even the physicists of today do not agree on many points. Scientists have the principles of uncertainty. Whether one goes to microcosm or macrocosm, there are uncertainties. Indicating Indra as gravitational force, the following hymns are relevant.

sakhā ha yatra sakhibhirnavaghvairabhijñvā satvabhirghā anughman |
satyaṃ tadindro dasabhirdaśaghbhiḥ sūryaṃ vivedatamasi kṣiyantam || (3.39.5)

When Indra started with nine horses and friendly Angiras in search of cows, he found Sun hidden in deep darkness and rescued the Sun. It is again mentioned that cow means light and Angiras means the luster of Agni. But why nine horses?

mā śūne aghne ni ṣadāma nṛṇāṃ māśeṣaso.avīratā paritvā |
prajāvatīṣu duryāsu durya || (7.1.11)

This hymn indicates the role of gravity in relation to the nuclear activity in sun's sphere giving rise to heat and light. Here the Gods are Sun, Etasha, Vayu, Indra, and Kutsa. Actually, they are not Gods, it is again being mentioned. Etasha may be some form of energy associated with atoms. Kutsa is electrical force.

Etasha is worshipper of Indra, so Indra treats him as a friend. In rivalry between the Sun, and Etasha, the great Indra helped Etasha, who offered Som to Indra. Etasha is also a favourite of Aswin Kumars.

Etasha is name of one of the horses of the Sun, different from the seven of day time. Etasha is one who brings the Sun from west to east. It is said that when Indra had stopped the movement of the Sun, Etasha was drawing the wheels of the Sun's chariot. Etasha appears to be a celestial body, a star or some force. It comes seventeen times in Ṛig-Veda.

asmin na indra pṛtsutau yaśasvati śimīvati krandasi prāvasātaye |
yatra ghoṣātā dhṛṣiteṣu khādiṣu viṣvakpatanti didyavo nṛṣāhye ||
(10.38.1)

The above hymn indicates that Indra (gravity) obstructs the movement of light. The effect of gravity was discussed by Einstein and was proved when the pull by Mercury was observed. Modern research in astronomy has indicated that light energy from distant stars does not travel in a straight line but seems to be deflected due to the effects of gravitational attraction.

sa sūryaḥ paryurū varāṃsyendro vavṛtyād rathyevacakrā |
atiṣṭhantamapasyaṃ na sarghaṃ kṛṣṇā tamāṃsitviṣyā jaghāna ||
(10.89.2)

Indra revolves celestial bodies in space. Griffith also means this. Three hymns, 10.119.9, 10 and 11 prove without doubt that Indra is force of gravity. Hymn 2.19.3 suggests that Indra causes the Sun and sun rays to appear.

Aditi is mother of Indra. Before breast feeding, she gave Indra the Som as suggested in the following hymn 3.48.2.

yajjāyathāstadaharasya kāme.aṃśoḥ pīyūṣamapibo ghiriṣṭhām|
taṃ te mātā pari yoṣā janitrī mahaḥ piturdama āsiñcadaghre||

It is mentioned that Indra made his body as per his wishes. He controls Dyulok (Sanskrit for galaxy) and Antariksha (earth). He produced the Sun. He is the only master of celestial Som. He keeps half of the Som for himself and the rest he gives to other Gods. Som will be introduced in the coming pages.

Indra's wives are Som, Sachi, and Indrani. Indra's son is Vasulkara Indra. He is Rishi of Mandala 10 Sukta 27. He is also as good a warrior as his father. Vasulkara means producer of Vasu. There are eight Vasus. In the context of the above hymn the meaning of Vasu will be Agni and also producer of rays. Right from the formation of particles, its consolidation is done by Indra and matter is produced. The energy in the matter thus produced is Vasu.

The entire sukta 27 of mandala 10 is of tremendous importance for researchers of Physics.

If Indra was born then as per the law of nature he must die. It is questionable as to how gravity can die. If one refers to the concept of Aakash and Pran for projection called creation and its subsidence called deluge, annihilation, or end of creation then after the end there will be no gravity. The observation of Rishi is not understandable that Indra just after his birth killed his father and spared mother Aditi.

There is God Kutsa, who is identical, clone type of Indra. As per hymn 4.16.10 below, Kutsa and Indra are so similar that Indra's wife Sachi could not distinguish.

ā dasyughnā manasā yāhy astam bhuvat te kutsaḥ sakhye nikāmaḥ |
sve yonau ni ṣadataṃ sarūpā vi vāṃ cikitsad ṛtacid dha nārī ||

Griffith has translated that Kutsa's wife could not distinguish. The reason is that in this hymn "the faithful lady could not distinguish when Indra brought his friend Kutsa at his residence."

Reverting back to the fact that Indra means gravitation force it is very much apparent that Kutsa means the electrical force. It suggests similarity between formulae of gravitation and electrical attraction or repulsion.

As per hymn 4.26.1 Kutsa is the son of Arjuni. Lord Krishna's words in the song celestial Gita are very much similar to this hymn. The supreme (Paramatma) says that he is Indra, Kutsa, Surya, Rishi, Kaksivan and Rishi Ushana. The importance of Kutsa is such that his name has come thirty-seven times in Ṛig-Veda. This perhaps indicates the importance of the laws of electricity.

The Rishis had found that gravity can be absorbed. In 36.32.1 Rishi Vishwamitra requests Indra to loosen his two horses so that they may have mouthful of food. Vishwamitra has indicated that the two horses or the waves can be made inactive. Gravity can be nullified by making a levitator highly charged by negative charge and as earth is negative charge, so by repulsion the effect of gravity can be neutralized. Translation of this hymn by Griffith is based on Sayan's translation that is bent towards spiritualism.

Indra is worshipped and known more as a warrior than for any other quality. When he was born, a lady demon tried to devour him but infant Indra drove her away. When Indra grew up he killed many demons. The most powerful among whom was Vritra. So, Indra is also called "Vritra Hanta" which means killer of Vritra. It is said that Vritra was withholding light and water. It is essential to know Astronomy in order to understand Vritra. The great freedom fighter of India—Bal Gangadhar Tilak, has explained Vritra in his book "The Arctic Home in the Vedas" from geographical, geological and astronomical points of view. (Please see Appendix-A on Vritra)

Among weapons of Indra, the Vajra or the thunder bolt is known as lightning striking this earth. As per 10.96.3 below, Indra's Vajra is Harit (the color of his horse) and is made of iron.

so asya vajro harito ya āyaso harirnikāmo harirāghabhastyoḥ |
dyumnī suśipro harimanyusāyaka indre ni rūpāharitā mimikṣire ||

divi na keturadhi dhāyi haryato vivyacad vajro harito naraṃhyā |
tudadahiṃ hariśipro ya āyasaḥ sahasraśokāabhavad dharimbharaḥ ||
(10.96.4)

The above hymn 10.96.4, is more interesting as it means that Vajra is as luminous as the Sun and is in the sky like Indra's horses. These hymns indicate meteorites as they are luminous, contain metals and loiter in the sky. Meteorites fall towards the earth due to gravitational force, whereas lightning is associated with electrical charges with which Indra's friends Kutsa can be associated.

Aswini Kumars

These are twins. Their name bears the word Ashwa which means horse. Their mother is Sangya, wife of Vivaswan who is one of the twelve Adityas (Sun). Adityas are sons of mother Aditi who is one of the thirteen wives of Kashyap. (The Appendix-G may be seen). It appears that the twins Aswins were trained in medicine. One was a physician while the other was a surgeon.

The Aswins represent beneficial forces or energies of nature abundant at the hours of sunrise, noon and at sunset. It is a subject of research as to what is meant by Aswins. Once discovered it would be a boon for humanity for leading a healthy life.

The importance of Aswini Kumars can be assessed by their appearance in the third sukta of the first mandala. This mandala is by Rishi Vishwamitra's son and starts with Agni (energy) in the first sukta. In the second sukta are Vayu Indra, Vayu Mitra, and Varun. The third starts with Aswini Kumar. Aswins are praised in this third sukta as a fast walker, doer of many jobs, keeper of patience and intelligence, killer of disease, always a speaker of truth, and ferocious like Rudra. Many of these merits are definitely essential for physicians and surgeons. The hymns in praise of these twins also refer to aircrafts.

trayaḥ pavayo madhuvāhane rathe somasya venām anu viśva id viduḥ |
traya skambhāsa skabhitāsa ārabhe trir naktaṃ yāthas trir v aśvinā divā ||
(1.34.2)

The Aswin's chariot with three wheels and three supports is designed to carry Som (or moon) for which Aswins have fascination. They travel with this chariot three times during day and three times at night. In this context, number three has got prominence. Aswins are requested to come three times a day—early morning, noon, and evening. In the morning, the twins give divine glowing medicines, at noon they provide terrestrial medicine, and in the evening they give watery medicines. according to hymn 1.34.6 given below. Aswins significance is guessed as medicines for Vayu (gas), Pitta (bile), and Kapha (phlegm) as per Ayurvedic system.

trir no aśvinā divyāni bheṣajā triḥ pārthivāni trir u dattam adbhyaḥ |
omānaṃ śaṃyor mamakāya sūnave tridhātu śarma vahataṃ śubhas
patī || (1.34.6)

yo vāmaśvinā manaso javīyān rathaḥ svaśvo viśa ājighāti |
yena ghachathaḥ sukṛto duroṇaṃ tena narā vartirasmabhyaṃ
yātam || (1.117.2)

The above hymn indicates that Aswins come with their chariots with a speed more than the speed of mind. The role of Aswins in the above hymn has not been clarified even by

Griffith. Referring to the speed of mind, Griffith translates it to be "swifter than thought".

Now, one can ask the scientific meaning of mind and thought. The great Indian, Swami Vivekananda has explained that the mind is a matter vibrating at nearly infinite frequency and that thought is a force. Because frequency is nearly infinite the speed is nearly infinite. Present-day science considers speed of light in a vacuum to be the maximum speed. But it is controversial. In Vedic texts the fastest is the mind. Descartes (the mathematician), Vidur (an intellectual of ancient India), and many others have tried to define mind and to assess where does it reside in a body. Descartes thinks that heart is the abode of mind. Vidur thinks that mind is in the entire body. According to Vidur's view mind is controlled by the moon, which controls blood and blood is in the entire body. In fact, this hymn is for research.

trivandhureṇa trivṛtā rathena tricakreṇa suvṛtā yātamarvāk |
pinvataṃ ghā jinvatamarvato no vardhayatamaśvinā vīramasme ll
(1.118.2)

In the above hymn also, the chariot of Aswins is indicated to be triangular in design. According to this hymn, Aswins give udderful cows (light, knowledge), horse (strength), and heroic children (sons, daughters or actions).

yuvaṃ dhenuṃ śayave nādhitāyāpinvatamaśvinā pūrvyāya |
amuñcataṃ vartikāmaṃhaso niḥ prati jaṅghāṃ viśpalāyā adhattam ||
(1.118.8)

You (Aswins) provided an artificial leg made of iron for Rishi Vispala whose one leg was broken. This indicates excellence in surgery during Vedic days.

The following hymn indicates that daughter of the Sun, Usha (the dawn), has accepted you (Aswins) as husband.

yuvoraśvinā vapuṣe yuvāyujaṃ rathaṃ vāṇī yematurasya śardhyam |
ā vāṃ patitvaṃ sakhyāya jaghmuṣī yoṣāvṛṇītajenyā yuvāṃ patī ||
(1.119.5)

aśvinorasanaṃ rathamanaśvaṃ vājināvatoḥ |
tenāhaṃ bhūri cākana || (1.120.10)

Aswins gave us military air planes without engines. These are glider planes. But Griffith has given spiritual meaning to this hymn. He admits that hymns of this sukta are difficult and obscure.

arvāṃ tricakro madhuvāhano ratho jīrāśvo aśvinoryātu suṣṭutaḥ |
trivandhuro maghavā viśvasaubhaghaḥ śaṃ na ā vakṣad dvipade catuṣpade || (1.157.3)

In the above hymn also the chariot of Aswins is triangular. As per this hymn the Aswins made his plane stationary over the ocean to save Vrijju, son of Tugna, who was drowning in the ocean. Does this refer to existence of helicopters?

Mandala 1 sukta 116, has descriptions of military weapons such as ships, submarines, modes of transporting water, and aircrafts high above in Antariksha. It contains knowledge of anti-aging drugs, eye treatment, artificial limbs, and rejuvenating the udder of dry cows. Key themes of some hymns are listed below.

Hymn 2: Super fast aircrafts.

Hymn 3: Antariksha planes, submarines, ships.

Hymn 4: Actions in desert, tank (hundred wheels and six horses) three air planes.

Hymn 5: Ocean ships.

Hymn 9: Canal construction and rejuvenating the udders of dry cows.

Hymn 10: Chavan Rishi's old age was turned into youth and he married a beautiful women.

Hymn 13: The intelligent women on a long travel. Aswins gave her a good son. This is translated by Griffith as a weakling's wife (Vadrimati). It suggests that a weak man's wife got a son, meaning that her husband was cured.

Hymn 14: Restoration of eyesight.

Hymn 15: Artificial iron leg provided to a king who was going for battle.

Hymn 16: Permanent restoration of eyesight.

Hymn 22: Drawing water from a very deep well.

Thus the entire sukta 116 of mandala 1 is highly informative. Hymns of Sukta 1-117 are equally meaningful and these should be read with Sukta 112. All these show the extent of advancement in the fields of medical science and military weapons.

yuvaṃ cid dhi ṣmāśvināvanu dyūn virudrasya prasravaṇasyasātau |
aghastyo narāṃ nṛṣu praśastaḥ kārādhunīva citayat sahasraiḥ ||
(1.180.8)

This hymn 1.180.8, indicated that dark clouds can be made to rain torrentially by music. Perhaps music here refers to some type of sound waves.

yuvametaṃ cakrathuḥ sindhuṣu plavamātmanvantaṃ
pakṣiṇantaughryāya kam |
yena devatrā manasā nirūhathuḥ supaptanīpetathuḥ kṣodaso
mahaḥ || (1.182.5)

The above hymn suggests existence of a hovercraft or hydroplane which lands and takes off from river or ocean.

prātaryāvāṇā rathyeva vīrājeva yamā varamā sacethe |
mene iva tanvā śumbhamāne dampatīva kratuvidā janeṣu || (2.39.2)

The hymn 2.39.2 refers to Aswins who come in the early morning hours like two warriors, like two women with beautiful bodies, like a pair of husband and wife.

This hymn indicates that Aswins come in the early morning hours, also known as the hours of Brahma (Brahma Bela). They come as warriors to kill diseases of a person who gets up early in the morning Aswins bring nature's beauty and softness all around (two women) and are as complementary to each other as husband and wife.

Before stating more about Aswins, it is worthwhile to state that existence of aircrafts, gliders, helicopters, hovercrafts during Vedic days are not just fanciful thoughts of the Rishis. In Ṛig-Veda there are hymns that confirm the existence of such crafts. In Atharwa Veda the details of air planes are given.

The hymn 1.25.7, 1.30.19 and 1.116.3 may be referred to for existence of aircrafts in Vedic days.

vedā yo vīnāṃ padamantarikṣeṇa patatām |
veda nāvaḥ samudriyaḥ || (1.25.7)

This hymn is addressed to God Varun, it means "he who knows way and path of birds that fly, he knows about air and sea crafts (aircrafts and ships)."

trir no aśvinā yajatā dive-dive pari tridhātu pṛthivīm aśāyatam |
tisro nāsatyā rathyā parāvata ātmeva vātaḥ svasarāṇi ghachatam ||
(1.34.7)

This hymn (1.34.7), indicated aircraft made of iron, copper and silver. This hymn refers to three types of vehicles for land, sea and air.

aritraṃ vāṃ divas pṛthu tīrthe sindhūnāṃ rathaḥ |
dhiyā yuyujra indavaḥ || (1.46.8)

The above hymn 1.46.8, indicates that such vehicles can cross oceans at high altitude. For these vehicles a pond of water should be made for providing water to the vehicle. Here water can mean hydrogen and oxygen. This hymn indicates rockets. Similar descriptions are given in hymn 1.85.4.

The translation of hymns 1.46.7, 1.164.46 and 1.164.48 by Swami Dayanand Saraswati are very clear about types and design of airplane. His book Rigvedadi Bhasya Bhumika may be referred. Swami Dayanand Saraswati, the founder of Arya Samaj, brought religious renaissance in the nineteenth century India. His book was written in 1876, years before the Wright brothers—Orville Write and Wilbur Write's first successful flight in 1903. Griffith's translation was published in 1889. Sharma's translation is of the period 1960. Dayanand was not just spiritual. He had an open mind and scientific approach. Sri Aurobindo has accepted Swami Dayanand's approach. The hymn 1.164.48, given below, is worth careful appraisal.

indraṃ mitraṃ varuṇamaghnimāhuratho divyaḥ sa suparṇo gharutmān |
ekaṃ sad viprā bahudhā vadantyaghniṃ yamaṃ ātariśvānamāhuḥ ||

The following are three different translations:

1. The simple translation is that "in a wheel there are twelve spokes, three axles, and 360 bolts. No man understands it."

2. According to Griffith, twelve are fellies in single wheel with three naves. They are set together with 360 spokes. The single wheel is year, the twelve spokes are months, the three naves are three seasons of four months each and 360 are the days of a year.

3. Swami Dayanand Saraswati has translated this hymn in detail. He has given designs of aircrafts. "There should be twelve supports and all instruments will be fitted on the support. There should be one wheel with which all instruments become functional. In the center of aircrafts there will be three wheels, one to stop, the other for forward movement and the third for backward movement. There should be 300 joints in the frame of the plane. There should be sixty instruments of which some should be in reserve and rest should function. When plane has to ascend the steam chamber be closed and when to descend the steam chamber should be open. When to move eastward the opening at east be closed and at west be opened, similarly, for north and south." Such operations need to be understood.

4. Regarding aircrafts and ships, Atharwa-Veda, an off-shoot of Ṛig-Veda and other books of the past may be studied such as Vymaanika Shastra by Maharishi Bharadwaj.

Reverting back to Aswini Kumars one can reason as to why applied science, and aeronautics are associated with Aswins. Perhaps their name "Ashwa" explains it since Ashwa means force, activity, quickness. The Rishis, perhaps, made Aswins a figurehead to tell secrets of medical and other applied sciences, and technologies.

Som

Som is not properly understood. People in general call alcohol as Somras (essence of Som). Some persons call Som a celestial wine. The Rishis have told in very plain words that Som is not wine. It is wave, frequency and that too cosmic. Som appears as early as the first hymn of the second sukta of the first mandala in association with Vayu. Then Som appears in the third sukta with Indra and Aswins.

Som is of such importance that out of ten mandalas of Ṛig-Veda, one complete mandala—the ninth, is predominantly for Som. This mandala is a treasure of information about Som.

Som is explained in two parts: firstly, as an energy from galaxy, and secondly, a drink made by extract of a creeper which absorbs Som.

Som can be understood and its properties realized by scholars of physics, astrophysics, and botany. It is beyond the reach of common man to understand Som. The first part, relevant to science, is introduced hereafter. Like Rishi Vishwamitra, member of his family Rishi Vamdeo has given truths of science in his hymn. He says that Som is "sweet intoxicating wave."

yuvaṃ tāsāṃ divyasya praśāsane viśāṃ kṣayatho
amṛtasyamajmanā |
yābhirdhenumasvaṃ pinvatho narā tābhir... || (1.112.3)

Som is born in Divyalok, which means the world of light may be galaxy, the nearest Milky Way.

indrāghnī ā ghataṃ sutaṃ ghīrbhirnabho vareṇyam |
asya pātaṃ dhiyeṣitā || (3.12.1)

The above hymn indicates that Som has come from sky.

upasthāya mātaramannamaiṭṭa tighmamapaśyadabhi somamūdhaḥ |
prayāvayannacarad ghṛtso anyān mahāni cakre purudhapratīkaḥ ||
(3.48.3)

Som existed when Indra was born. Indra's mother Aditi fed him Som before her breast milk. Since Indra appears to be a representation of gravitational force, this hymn means that Som can be ingested by gravitational force. It also means that Som strengthens gravitational force.

nṛṇāmu tvā nṛtamaṃ ghīrbhirukthairabhi pra vīramarcatā sabādhaḥ|
saṃ sahase purumāyo jihīte namo asya pradiva eka īśe|| (3.51.4)

Indra is the only owner of Som in the sky.

bharad yadi vir ato vevijānaḥ pathoruṇā manojavā asarji |
tūyaṃ yayau madhunā somyenota śravo vivide śyeno atra ||(4.26.5)

The falcon Shyen brought Som from Divyalok – world of light, the galaxy. The falcon Shyen is to be understood. It has importance in Ṛig-Veda. Most probably, falcon personifies high speed and accuracy at target.

drapsaścaskanda prathamānanu dyūnimaṃ ca yonimanu yaśca purvaḥ |
samānaṃ yonimanu saṃcarantaṃ drapsaṃ juhomyanu sapta hotrāḥ || (10.17.11)

Somras was born in Antariksha for Rishis and Gods.

somaṃ manyate papivan yat sampiṃṣantyoṣadhim |
somaṃ yambrahmāṇo vidurna tasyāśnāti kaścana || (10.85.3)

All are not capable of drinking Som by mouth. This Som is known only to Rishis and enlightened persons. It is said that cosmic energy is absorbed by Rishis through their frontal lobe. This kept Rishi from hunger, weakness and disease.

somenādityā balinaḥ somena pṛthivī mahī |
athonakṣatrāṇāmeṣāmupasthe soma āhitaḥ || (10.85.2)

All Gods like Adityas are strong only because of Som. Som is also amidst the constellations.

ete vātā ivoravaḥ parjanyasyeva vṛṣṭayaḥ |
aghneriva bhramā vṛthā || (9.22.2)

Som travelled at the speed of flame of fire. This obviously means velocity of light.

vṛṣṇaste vṛṣṇyaṃ śavo vṛṣā vanaṃ vṛṣā madaḥ |
satyaṃ vṛṣan vṛṣedasi || (9.64.2)

Som comes in cosmic showers.

ete asṛghramāśavo.ati hvarāṃsi babhravaḥ |
somā ṛtasya dhārayā || (9.63.4)

High speed Som of grey color moves with Jala or water stream. But in 9.19.3 Som is of green color.

trirasmai sapta dhenavo duduhre satyāmāśiraṃ pūrvye vyomani |
catvāryanyā bhuvanāni nirṇije cārūṇi cakre yad ṛtairavardhata ||
(9.70.1)

Som is in Param Vyom. Pram Vyom has been explained earlier as the "highest heaven."

pari suvāno hariraṃśuḥ pavitre ratho na sarji sanaye hiyānaḥ |
āpacchlokamindriyaṃ pūyamānaḥ prati devānajuṣata prayobhiḥ ||
(9.92.1)

Like a Rath or chariot, Som moves. It means, Som is a carrier. Perhaps this means modulation such as the principle on which radio waves carry sound waves. There are three types of modulations—phase, frequency, amplitude. The amplitude is for long range, the frequency modulation is for short range.

te.avadan prathamā brahmakilbiṣe.akūpāraḥ salilomātariśvā |
vīḷuharāstapa ughro mayobhūrāpo devīḥprathamajā ṛtena ||
(10.109.1)

The above hymn is highly scientific suggesting cerain aspects of the origin of the solar system that are not yet proven by the modern science. Griffith has not properly translated this hymn. According to this hymn, first Ap came into existence at the time of creation, then Som and lastly Jal. These three taken in a combination of two at a time have created gravitational force, nuclear force and electromagnetic force, as understood by the Vedic scholars.

The study of relevant hymn indicates that Jal means plasma, Som is frequency, but Ap has to be understood. The entire sukta 30 of the tenth mandala is for Ap. The God of this sukta is Ap or Apanpat.

Apanpat is represented as fast moving. In oceans Apanpat is encircled by water, shines brightly without fuel. Is it something like phosphors? In surroundings of water, he drinks for the first time the nectar from ocean. From him is born Ashwa (horse), his cows can be easily milked, he the Ap, the immortal, very large and lives in water and is bright all around; lives as electricity in clouds. His color is golden. His eyes are golden and he lives in a golden place. These descriptions are for Ap.

Griffith translates Apanpat as son of water—a name of Agni as "born in the form of lightning from the water of the aerial ocean or firmament." He thinks about origin of the Sun from Apanpat. For Griffith, Apanpat is Agni and dwells inside water.

nidhīyamānamapaghūḷamapsu pra me devānāṃ vratapāuvāca |
indro vidvānanu hi tvā cacakṣa tenāhamaghneanuśiṣṭa āghām ||
(10.32.6)

Agni is inside Jala or Ap. This is known to Indra.

imaṃ vidhanto apāṃ sadhasthe paśuṃ na naṣṭaṃ padairanu ghman |
ghuhā catantamuśijo namobhirichanto dhīrābhṛghavo.avindan ||
(10.46.2)

Ap has been searched out by Rishis and intellectual members of Bhrigu family, from the cave of water (Bhrigu means Sun's rays.)

mahat tadulbaṃ sthaviraṃ tadāsīd yenāviṣṭitaḥpraviveśithāpaḥ |
viśvā apaśyad bahudhā te aghne jātavedastanvo deva ekaḥ ||
(10.51.1)

The large body of Agni is encircled by Ap. From the above information about the Ap it appears that Ap means nuclear energy when associated with Jal which is plasma or atomic nucleus free from electrons.

apsarā jāramupasiṣmiyāṇā yoṣā bibharti parame vyoman |
carat priyasya yoniṣu priyaḥ san sīdat pakṣe hiraṇyayesa venaḥ ||
(10.123.5)

This hymn means Apsara (a nymph), born from Ap. Her husband is God Ven. This hymn is challenging and thought provoking. Who is this God Ven? From the root of word Ven, it means one who is loved by all. Ven is associated with Aditya, Atma, and Indra. According to Griffith, Ven is the loving sun. Ven is apparently the Sun as he rises amidst mist and dew in the morning. According to Griffith, Apsara is a celestial nymph who symbolizes the waters of heaven. Her lover is

Ven, the Gandharva, and the Sun. The hymn above (10.123.5), illustrates the two processes in which sun is brought in connection with water.

1. As penetrating with his (sun's) beams the watery masses of the sky; and,

2. In the assimilation of his (sun's) light with the waters, as Som or ambrosia. This association is stereotyped in union of Gandharva and the Apsara.

This hymn, says Griffith, is one of the most obscure in Ṛig-Veda. Various scholars have interpreted Ven in various manners. For example, according to Mahindhara, Ven means the Moon. Wilson interpreted it to be thundercloud, while Von Roth and Grossman think Ven to be Gandharva and the rainbow. Ludwig thinks Ven is the Moon and Gandharva is the Sun.

A critical examination will show that understanding Ap as water is wrong. Both are different and the triad is Ap, Som and Jal according to chronology of birth. So, Ap is different from Jal (water).

However, Ap is generally understood as Jal (water). Some thinks Ap as quantum state of matter. The hymn 10.32.6, referred to earlier, differentiates between Ap and Jal. The concept of quantum state developed in the last century. Thanks to Rishis like Einstein and Max Planck, a common person can understand the microscopic world of quantum. Generally, thoughts are tuned with visible world so microscopic world can be realized only by deep concentration, meditation, which leads to scientific research.

Ap is the master of smaller than the smallest, invisible and difficult to understand. Som is wave frequency. These two are understood as Aakash and Pran, Ether and Force—the two that cause projection (creation) of universe. From invisible state of Aakash, visible objects appear like Jal plasma, followed by galaxies, stars, planets, and satellites. This is Vedic concept. In the tenth mandala, various hymns reveal the process and cause of creation.

Reverting back to Som, there are many hymns which explain Som as follows:

1. Som creates Sun for light (9.3.12) and controls Sun (9.26.2)

2. Som creates constellation (9.42.1) in world of light and Sun to influence cows (rays) and Jal.

3. The hymn (9.66.2) is worth realizing. As per this hymn Pavanman Som settles in the west. Griffith has not explained this hymn. This hymn is understood with the facts that Som is unaffected by the rotation or revolution or gravitational force of this earth. The earth rotates from west to east so the stay of the Som seems to be in the west. Does it mean that Som comes from the east?

4. The Som appears in a vast zone in sky like the Sun. (9.71.7). Som particularly is bright at dawn.

5. The suktas 74 and 75 of the ninth mandala are highly scientific. The hymn 9.75.86 is equally scientific.

6. Due to Som, Sun is seen for a long period of time (9.1.6). As per hymn 31 of this mandala, the brightness of Sun is due to Som.

7. As per 9.98.5, Som lives with sun rays. Does it mean that Som is frequency?

8. As per 9.106.11, Som lives in high sky, vegetation and human being.

9. As per 9.108.14, Som is taken by Indra, Marut, Aryama, and Bhag, Mitra, Varun (last four are names of the Sun).

10. As per 9.110.3, through rays, Som maintains life in sky and on the earth. By his own capability he created Sun in the sky full of Jal. Here, obviously, Jal is solar fuel.

11. The 9.112 is riddle-like. The first hymn—"as a carpenter wishes for wood work, physician wishes for patients, priest wishes for someone willing Yagya, similarly human minds wishes for various desires as men's jobs are various. "

12. The hymn 10.16.6 is very puzzling. This, according to Griffith refers to partially-burnt corpse in a cremation place. This hymn is addressed to a dead person. "If your body has got pain from crows, ants, snakes, or any other killer animals then Agni, who eats all, will relieve you from pain. The nourishing Som in your body will also relieve you from pain." In this hymn Som has a different meaning than mentioned earlier. In Sanskrit, Som also means air. So, the Som of this hymn is the gas which starts forming inside the body after death to start the process of decomposition and helps quick burning of the corpse.

The second part about Som is the drink which was consumed by Rishis. The drink Somras (juice of Som) was for high growth of intellect. This drink was very different from alcohol. Scholars of Botany can assist in researching the herb from which Rishis obtained the Som through various processes, mixing of water, milk, and filtration through hair of sheep or ewes. It is for veterinarians to understand why sheep-wool was used.

According to Griffith, the Somras was juice of Moon Plant which was available on certain mountains. This plant has remained unidentified even today. Some scholars have suggested that the plant Som is "Ephedra Pachyclada".

The Vedic name of the Som plant is Somvalli. As per 9.113.3 "the daughter of Sun—Usha, has brought Som purified by rain water from Antariksha; it has been absorbed by Vasus and then established in the plant Somvalli." It suggests that Usha brings Som, meaning Som comes during early morning also known as the hour of Bhag. Som is purified by rain . It comes from Antariksha. Som is absorbed by Vasus and then established in Somvalli—the Som plant. Does this refer to photosynthesis? The Som plant grows on hills. As per 5.85.2 the Som creeper grows on the clefts of stones on mountains. This is the interpretation by an Indian translator Mahindhra and quoted by Griffith.

vaneṣu vy antarikṣaṃ tatāna vājam arvatsu paya usriyāsu |
hṛtsu kratuṃ varuṇo apsv aghniṃ divi sūryam adadhāt somam adrau || (5.85.2)

This hymn indicates that Somvalli is a creeper and is planted by Varun. Earlier, Varun has been explained as an infinitely vast expanse of water vapor in the universe. This hymn also means that Varun's influence increases strength in men and horses and equips cows with milk. It strengthens determination of heart, digestive power of stomach, establishes Sun in the world of light and Som on the mountains. It means that Som and Varun are related. In hymn 1.18.1 Griffith understands that Som drink gives inspiration and the drinkers are guided by tradition. As per hymn 4.42.6 Som juice makes one joyful.

sa ghā vīro na riṣyati yamindro brahmaṇas patiḥ |
somo hinoti martyam || (1.18.4)

This hymn means that he, who is inspired by Indra, Brihaspati, and Som, is never weakened. Indra is the organizing strength, Brihaspati is the guiding strength, and Som is the nourishing strength. Griffith's interpretation of the above hymn seems superior to that given by Indians scholars. Griffith has quoted professor William Whitney who believed that the Aryans knew that the juice of Som plant could elevate one's spirit under the influence of which a juice drinker was capable of deeds beyond natural powers. Aryans considered this juice as divine. Griffith has also quoted Max Muller, according to whom "we have no poetical words to express the high state of mental excitement produced by drinking the intoxicating juice of the Som." The state of excitement was celebrated as blessing of Gods and as a state in which both the warrior and the poet would reach their highest achievement.

Summarizing above interpretations one can conclude that Somras from Somavalli plant was much different from alcohol. Somras inspired good thoughts, gave eloquence, excitement, concentration to listen to and the power to present highly intelligent ideas in simple words. They spoke in coded words and gave facts many as yet not known to scientists in particular and public in general.

Scholars of Botany can understand the Somvalli plant. Modern science needs to research such divine plant as Somvalli. In the land of Veda, plants like Bhang (liquid derivative of Cannabis), Ganja (Cannabis Sahiva), and Dhatura (Thorn Apple) are known and are offered by some to Lord Shiva. No insult can be more serious than such offers to Lord Shiva. He is the calm and serene face of Rudra of Ṛig-Veda. Lord Shiva is complete silence (in meditation) unique (none is similar to him) the Fourth (which means the fourth state of mind-Turiya state, which is above awake, sleep and dreaming state) and He is Atma (the spirit) a part of the infinite, the Absolute. In the land of Veda, Lord Shiva has been wrongly associated with Bhang, Ganja and Dhatura.

Surya

In the hierarchy among Gods, Surya or Sun follows after Indra, Som, and Varun. Surya appears for the first time in Ṛig-Veda in hymn 1.7.3 much later than other Gods.

indro dīrghāya cakṣasa ā sūryaṃ rohayad divi |
vi ghobhiradrimairayat || (1.7.3)

As per this hymn Indra established Surya in high sky for lighting the world and Surya by his rays, made objects like mountains visible.

For all animate or inanimate objects of this earth, Surya (Sun) is the parent and hence the most kind. Like a parent, Surya offers everything that is good at every hour of day and night. Individuals who do not understand Him become victims of disease. He cures tuberculosis, eye defects, skin disease, heart problems and other ailments. His most kind nature is known to them who get up from bed about one hour earlier to His arrival in the east. This is the period when He, as Bhag-Savita, showers nectar on everything through His rays visible and invisible.

Hymns 1.50.9 and 10 very clearly point out seven visible colors (VIBGYOR) in sun rays thousands of years before Newton, by representing them as seven horses of the Sun's chariot.

ayukta sapta śundhyuvaḥ sūro rathasya naptyaḥ |
tābhiryāti svayuktibhiḥ || (1.50.9)
ud vayaṃ tamasas pari jyotiṣ paśyanta uttaram |
devaṃ devatrā sūryamaghanma jyotiruttamam || (1.50.10)

As per Griffith, the seven horses are the seven daughters of the Sun. From this seven number are derived the seven days of a week. But there is no mention elsewhere that Surya has seven daughters.

1.105.9 hymn more specifically indicates seven rays.

amī ye sapta raśmayastatrā me nābhirātatā |
tritastad vedāptyaḥ sa jāmitvāya rebhati vittame asya rodasi ||
(1.105.9)

Ludwing interprets the seven rays as the seven flames of Agni.

amī ye pañcokṣaṇo madhye tasthurmaho divaḥ |
devatrā nu pravācyaṃ sadhrīcīnā ni vāvṛturvittanme asya rodasi ||
(1.105.10)

The five powerful Gods—Agni, Sun, Moon, Vayu and Indra control the five organs of senses (Indriyas). As per Sayana, the five are—Indra, Varun, Agni, Aryaman, and Savita.

tan mitrasya varuṇasyābhicakṣe sūryo rūpaṃ kṛṇute dyorupasthe |
anantamanyad ruśadasya pājaḥ kṛṣṇamanyad dharitaḥ saṃ bharanti || (1.115.5)

This hymn says that due to the Sun there is day at one side of the earth and night on the other side. Griffith interprets that Sun is maker and ruler of day and night. But this hymn also indicates the shape of the earth.

prātaratne prātaritwa dadhati tacikitwan prāntigrihya ni dhante |
tena praja vardhyaman aryurayasposena sacete suvira ||
(1.125.1)

Hymn 1.125.1 suggests that the morning Sun gives health, and nourishing benefits. Prudent persons receive and entertain morning Sun, who gives long life, good child and wealth similar to the well-known proverb—early to bed and early to rise makes a man healthy, wealthy and wise.

te māyino mamire supracetaso jāmī sayonī mithunā samokasā |
navyaṃ-navyaṃ tantumā tanvate divi samudre antaḥ kavayaḥ
sudītayaḥ || (1.159.4)

Surya is posited in the world of light which is galaxy, and sends new rays every day. Why new rays? These rays, like sisters born from the same womb, are from the Sun. Griffith translated galaxy as the aerial ocean or atmosphere.

The entire sukta 164 of the first mandala is very thought provoking and essential to understanding Surya. It deals with seasons and activities of the Sun. In hymn 1 of this sukta (164) the handsome Surya, with his seven sons, has been mentioned. His middle brother is Vayu, who resides in mid-Antariksha and the third brother is Agni who has a brilliant back.

Griffith's translation is different. He thinks there are seven priests instead of seven sons and as per Griffith, the second brother is lightning and the third brother is Agni.

This hymn 16 of sukta 164 mandala 1, is very mysterious. According to this hymn, the rays of the Sun are feminine still they are male. This fact can be realized by keen and minute observations. Those who realize it can know the father of the father, as stated in this hymn. Griffith interprets that Surya (the Sun), is the father of the rays that bring rains and initiate this earth's activities (after rain), therefore, Surya is the father of the father.

All hymns of mandala 8 sukta 91 are by Apala, daughter of Rishi Atri. She suffered from skin disease and hence was deserted by her husband. She went to her father's house and worshipped Surya. She was cured. There are other interpretations of this episode of Apala, but they are spiritual.

In the fifth and sixth hymns of this sukta, there is clear mention of mental strength, high fertility of land and also fertility in women's womb all due to the Sun (Surya).

Overall, the eighth mandala refers to disease curing properties of the Sun's rays.

8.12.9 says that as Agni reduces jungles to ash, so by Sun's rays all our grief and enemies are burnt.

In 8.19.22 there is prayer to Aditya to increase longevity of persons destined for short life. It means that aging can be slowed by utilizing Sun's rays. The following hymns of the ninth mandala highlight significant benefits of the Sun.

> 9.10.8 Eyes are dependent on Sun.
>
> 9.75.1 Sitting on Sun's chariot Som becomes the observer of the world.
>
> 9.97.31 and 41 The Sun has his brightness from Som.
>
> 9.98.5 Sun rays are with Som.
>
> 10.158.3 Prayer to Savita (morning Sun) for superior eyesight.

Sukta 10.189 is thought provoking. According to Griffith's translation "the spotted bull hath come." This sukta 10.189 is for Surya and the spotted bull means Surya. For a common man Sun is not a bull and also cannot be spotted. And there are many such hymns of science which are not understood by common man and that is why Veda is called by them as shepherd's song.

Bull means great power. Those who have knowledge of Astronomy know that the Sun has spots which appear at certain intervals. The appearance of the sun-spots is associated with strong effects on the earth's atmosphere causing interference with power supply and communication.

Rishi of this hymn—Srparagee, is a Goddess. She is also the queen mother of Kadru, the serpent. This Rishi has appeared only once in Ṛig-Veda. This hymn's three mantras are regarding Surya. Perhaps this Rishi had observed the sun-spots.

The meaning of a serpent is normally not known. Serpent has hidden power in a soft state residing in the body as "Kundalini". A snake has a very soft body, but when the snake makes coil around any living body, tremendous pressure is exerted which could break the bones of its victim. So, Sun may also be considered as a snake because of its tremendous force not yet understood.

The Rishis knew the powers of the Sun specially beneficiary power of Bhag-Savita, the rising Sun and that is why the well known Gayatri, "Om bhurbhuwa Swah, tat saviturvareṇyaṃ bhargho devasya dhīmahi | dhiyo yo naḥ pracodayāt ||" in praise of Savita is being chanted since thousands of years.

Sun's wife is said to be Usha (dawn) but she is also said to be his daughter. Sun has a less known daughter Suryaa, who is said to be sister of Pusa who is one of the twelve Aditya as explained in Appendix G. If Pusa, the Aditya, is de-personified then he appears to be Sun, just after Bhag-Savita stage, after a little ascending sky in the east.

Sun's daughter, Suryaa's marriage is the ideal for Aryans marriage customs. A complete long sukta is for Suryaa's marriage. To know the meaning of husband and wife, the hymn 85 of the tenth mandala dealing with Suryaa's marriage has to be thoroughly understood. The 47 mantras (hymns) lay down the rules and principles of Aryan marriage. This deals with the proper type of marriage among the eight Adityas. The Adityas are sons of Aditi and are listed in Appendix-F (Daksha).

The hymn 10.85.36 indicates togetherness of husband and wife. Both complement and provide support to each other. They are like two pillars standing a little distance apart and having a beam of load (responsibility of the family) over them.

If Surya or Sun is understood as nature's power of fertility then fertility's first master is Som which means the Sun's rays, direct and also reflected from the moon. Som gave brightness and energy to the Sun's rays which is understood as Gandharva. From Som fertility comes to earth's soil and also to humans. The power to utilize fertility is the Aswins. Lastly there is the energy which is represented by Agni.

Gandharva is considered as a God who protects virgins. He also protects Som. After a girl is married Gandharva goes to another virgin to provide her the protection.

Gandharva appears in 1.22.14.

tayorid ghṛtavat payo viprā rihanti dhītibhiḥ |
ghandharvasya dhruve pade || (1.22.14)

This is hymn is very thought provoking. In between the sky and the earth, the two poles of the world of Gandharva, exists rich nourishment—the Jal, which is obtained by prudent persons by efforts. Griffith's translation indicates that Gandharvas are singers.

In hymn 3.38.6 Griffith translates Gandharvas as Indra. In hymn 9.113.3 Gandharva is referred to as guardian of heavenly Som.

Sukta 10.95 presents the conversation between Pururwa and Urvashi. In this story, Gandharva played a villain's role by stealing Urvashi's rams. Gandharvas created lightning and Urvashi saw Pururwa.

In 10.136.6 the Rishi says that the Sun travels in the worlds of Apsara, and Gandharvas. Gandharvas are also known as Vivasbasu (one of the Vasus) who live in the world of air and guard Som. The Sun is called Gandharva. The rain cloud is also called Gandharva. The Moon is called Gandharva. In 10.126 there is a reference of Gaur, a wild buffalo whose leg is white just above ankle. Vasu have delivered this Gaur from Vivasbasu, the Gandharva.

The Gandharvas, although an object of nature, got importance because of the Gandharva-Veda, which came much later after the first four Vedas and established a musical tradition of ragas.

The Gandharva word also became familiar as a class of people who called themselves Gandharva. They were people of simple lifestyle, fond of music and dance but they were brave warriors who ultimately became friends of Arjun.

Chandra

The God Chandra (Moon), also known as Chandrama, appears in the tenth mandala of sukta 10.85.19. Earlier this God has appeared many times by the name Som.

navo-navo bhavati jāyamāno.ahnāṃ keturuṣasāmetyaghram |
bhāghaṃ devebhyo vi dadhātyāyan pra
candramāstiratedīrghamayuḥ || (10.85.19)

In 10.85.19 the Rishis says that Chandra is new at every rising in the sky. He gives blissful life and long age. In hymn 18 of this sukta, Sun and Moon are called the two children. The Moon creates seasons and rises and sets again and again. In hymn 5 of the same, Som (Chandra) shapes years and months. As per Griffith, Gods drink Som when the Moon is waning.

As per 10.90.13, Chandra is born out of the mind of Virat Purush and Sun is born out of his eyes.

candramā manaso jātaścakṣoḥ sūryo ajāyata |
mukhādindraścāghniśca prāṇād vāyurajāyata || (10.90.13)

This sukta of Virat Purush is highly scientific as a whole. Virat means gigantic, enormous and Purush means man. By Virat Purush, the Rishi conceived of a person of infinite size who controls everything of this universe both animate and inanimate. The past creation, the existing creation, and the future creation are all by the Virat Purush.

To understand Virat Purush one needs a highly elevated intellect. In hymn 15 of this sukta (90) there is reference of electron and periodic table of elements.

Since Chandra is in the mind of Virat Purush it is also interpreted that the mind of man (or woman) is controlled by Moon. Special effects of full moon and new moon are on the brains and mind. The word lunatic has come from Lunar which means Moon. The hymns also indicate that moon light is the reflected light of Sun. All medical herbs are controlled by the Moon.

For poets and writers, Chandra (Moon) is the most beloved. It is said that while planets and satellites were under formation, a chunk from the earth came out and later on became Moon. It is based on the evidence that volume of the Pacific Ocean is nearly equal to the volume of the Moon. This is for astronomers to accept or deny. There is one story about Moon as a casanova. (Please see Appendix-B)

Brihaspati

The earlier Vedic name of Brihaspati is Brahmanaspati. The planet Jupiter is said as Guru or Brihaspati. He is the God of prayer and teacher of all Gods, so he is often called Guru. The word Guru means heavy as well as remover of darkness or ignorance.

Brahmanaspati or Brihaspati is said to be handsome like Agni and Mitra (midday Sun). He protects his worshippers from problems, and enemies.

God Brihaspati appears first in 1.14.3 with Vayu, Agni, Indra Vayu, Mitra, Pusa, Bhag and all Maruts.

indravāyū bṛhaspatiṃ mitrāghniṃ pūṣaṇaṃ bhagham |
ādityānmārutaṃ ghaṇam || (1.14.3)

Indra-Vayu is the energy for breathing. Maruts will be explained later. In 1.18.1 and 3, Brihaspati is said to be owner of all knowledge, prosperity, remover of disease, bestowal of riches, giver of good health and one who can be easily pleased. According to Griffith, "in Brihaspati the action of worshiper upon God is personified. Brihaspati is the supplant, the priest who intercedes with Gods for men and protects them against the wicked. He appears as the prototype of the priests and its order and he is also designated as the purohit (Sanskrit for chief priest) of all divine community. The essential difference between the original idea represented in this God and those expressed in most of the other and older deities of Veda consisted in the fact that the later are personifications of various departments of nature or of physical forces, while the former is the product of moral idea and impersonation of the power of division."

In the war with cow-lifters, according to Aurobindo, Brihaspati is more frequently the hero of the victory. Brihaspati coming first into birth from the great light in the supreme ether, as seven-mouthed, multiple-born, seven-rayed is one who dispels darkness. In this context hymns 4.50.4 and 5 be seen.

The sukta 73 of the sixth mandala has only three hymns as follows, all for Brihaspati.

yo adribhit prathamajā ṛtāvā bṛhaspatirāṅghiraso haviṣmān |
dvibarhajmā prāgharmasat pitā na ā rodasī vṛṣabho roravīti ||
janāya cid ya īvata u lokaṃ bṛhaspatirdevahūtau cakāra |
ghnan vṛtrāṇi vi puro dardarīti jayañchatrūnramitrān pṛtsu sāhan ||
bṛhaspatiḥ samajayad vasūni maho vrajān ghomato deva eṣaḥ |
apaḥ siṣāsan svarapratīto bṛhaspatirhantyamitramarkaiḥ ||

He is the hill-breaker, the first-born, the Angiras. Brihaspati is also an Angiras and one who becomes Angiras. In this context, 6.73.1, 10.47.6, 2.23.18 may be referred to.

Angiras is in the first place a power of Agni. He is the seer who works by the light, by the knowledge. He is the flame of the puissance of Agni, the great force that is born into the world to be the priest of Yagya and the leader of journey.

With reference to Brihaspati the meaning of first-born, seven-mouthed, and seven-rayed need to be researched. Perhaps Astronomy can explain it if Brihaspati is taken as the planet Jupiter. It is well known that among planets Jupiter is the heaviest (Guru). The first-born may be the first planet which came into existence. The great light may be the nebulae from which Sun and other planets came into existence. The seven-mouthed may be the seven satellites of Jupiter that the Rishis knew about and the different radiations from them are the seven rays. Perhaps the Rishis suggested that the great planet Jupiter by its gravity protects earth from wanderers such as comets, and meteorites.

Rishis in their state of super consciousness framed mantras by selecting words and simple examples with suitable metres for melodious singing. The hymns have five dimensions which includes effect of sound waves emanating from the metres and words for the good of the listeners.

This subtle super-consciousness is Brahmin which does not mean a caste. Anybody, in deep meditation can achieve this state. The word Brahmin has also been defined by Lord Krishna in the book Bhagvat Gita. There has been metamorphosis in the word Brahmanaspati to Brihaspati to Brahma—one of the triad Brahma, Vishnu, Mahesh.

Brihaspati's wife is Juhu and she was restored to her husband by Som. Gods Mitra, and Varun, approved of the restoration. Gods praised Juhu as chaste and asked Brihaspati to hold her hand. The seven Rishis and other Gods made declaration of this union of husband and wife. The Gods said that the wife is very resourceful and is in Param Vyom. She has power that is not available easily. Because Brihaspati had deserted his wife Juhu who was a pious lady, all Gods considered Brihaspati a sinner. After he accepted Juhu, his sin was pardoned.

This story reflects upon the creation of the solar family. Perhaps Juhu represents the largest satellite of Jupiter. Because of the fluctuations in the gravitational force, the satellite was drawing towards the Sun, but eventually it came within the gravitational field of Jupiter.

This story has a different meaning in spiritualism, Juhu is also known as Vak. In Sanskrit, Vak means word, speech, the origin of speech, and Saraswati. Vak resides in Param Vyom. Brihaspati is also called Vakpati meaning husband of Vak who is also known as divine speech (Divya Vani). Vak is daughter of Rishi Ambhum (1.164.45). It is mentioned that in spiritualism there are different kinds of speech- Param, Pashyanti, Madhyama, Baikhari. Param means beyond and this param speech is Divya Vani. The conversation between persons of Param is not audible to others and they may be seated at large distances. Perhaps these four types are related to the frequency of waves. If frequency is low then amplitude is larger. Waves with large amplitude can travel to large distances as they overcome obstruction in the path of propagation. If frequency is high, then amplitude is small hence waves get scattered while in movement. Perhaps Rishis knew this art of communication at a very low frequency. Normal human beings sound waves are scattered. The meaning of word baikhari is scattered.

Rudra

Among the three fundamental Gods, one is Rudra, whose common name is Mahadev, Mahesh, or Shiva. In appearance, actions of Rudra are fearsome and violent but in effect they are beneficial. For example, volcanoes cause damage for a short period of time but in due course they give fertility to soil. Forest fires ultimately give healthy vegetation. Lightning during thunderstorms produces nitrous oxide that adds to the fertility of soil. The word Rudra, according to its root, means blood red. Perhaps life started in volcanic zone under Rudra. The concept of Rudra is a little difficult to understand. Lord Shiva (Rudra) also kown as Natraj (king of dancers) had once danced a violent dance called Tandav dance at the creation of this universe. Rudra's Tandav was because his wife Gauri (Parvati), committed suicide due to humiliation of Lord Shiva by her father Daksha.

There are eleven Rudras. Even thirty-three Rudras are believed to exist. Perhaps each of the eleven has been subdivided into three. May be it suggests Rudra's association with thirty three sub-atomic particles.

Rudra is considered a protector of animals, so his name is Pashupati, which means Lord of animals. Rudra is sometimes referred to as Rudragan which means Rudra with followers.

Rudra's sons Maruts are well-known. Marut means strong wind power. Their mother is Prishni. Maruts are associated with Goddesses Rodasi and Saraswati. In the army of Gods, Maruts are always in the forefront. Maruts are good friends of Indra and they assisted Indra for killing Vritra. As per 8.96.9 there are 63 Maruts with Indra. Maruts with followers are called Marutgan.

Rodasi is lightning personified and and according to some she is wife of the total group of Maruts. She is also treated as a Goddess who presides over childbirth, might be the intense labor pain.

As stated earlier, Prishni is wife of Rudra and mother of Maruts. Prishni means cow (light). Rudra is said to be God of water meaning firmament, as Aditya is God of heaven and God of earth are the Vasu. Taking into account all the views about Rodasi, it appears that Rodasi and Prishni are lightning personified. Among the eleven Rudras, one is lightning.

Maruts, being sons of Rudra, are as ferocious as Rudra. For example, earthquake is violent and so is the pyroclasts, the storm (Marut) containing volcanic ash moving at the speed of more than 600km/hour at the time of volcanic eruption.

The Maruts is not the wind or storm associated with rains caused by Indra as commonly understood. When Indra is depersonified as gravitational or electromagnetic waves, then Maruts are different than storms. Flow of electrons at a fast speed may also be a type of Maruts. Maruts are subtle. The solar storms which disrupt communication and even power supply are also Maruts. Lightning is Rudra. Agni and Rudra are associated.

tamoṣadhīrdadhire gharbhaṃ ṛtviyaṃ tamāpo aghnimjanayanta mātaraḥ |
tamit samānaṃ vaninaśca vīrudho'ntarvatīśca suvate ca viśvahā ||
(10.91.6)

As per the above hymn, Agni is produced in the form of lightning by the water of the firmament or the clouds and descends with the rain into plants, trees and vegetation in general.

Rudra's sons Marut know vegetation as per hymn 8.20.25. Rishis, the worshippers of nature, personified vegetation as God Vanaspati who appears in 1.13.11 for the first time.

ava sṛjā vanaspate deva devebhyo haviḥ |
pra dāturastu cetanam || (1.13.11)

With reference to Maruts, sukta 8.94 is worth understanding. As per hymn 7 of this sukta Maruts are born by reverse movement. This needs explanation by scientists.

Hymns 8.20.4 and 5 very clearly present scenes at volcanic eruptions and the tremor of earth, and pyroclastic storms.

Griffith has not translated these properly. But Shayan's translation indicates it to be coastal waves. Hymn 8 of this sukta indicates that Maruts play Veena (the musical instrument of Goddess Saraswati). Marut's movement is serpentine, they protect oceans. This complete sukta is for research.

The suktas 77 and 78 of the tenth mandala are highly scientific. Sukta 77 hymn 2 indicates that Maruts affect gravity and also terrestrial magnetism. Sukta 78 indicates origin of Maruts from one source. Griffith and Shayan have interpreted it from the point of rituals and spiritualism.

According to hymn 10.99.2 Maruts move with Indra to conquer enemies.

sa hi dyutā vidyutā veti sāma pṛthuṃ yonimasuratvāsasāda |
sa sanīḷebhiḥ prasahāno asya bhrāturna ṛtesaptathasya māyāḥ ||
(10.99.2)

Ribhus

Like Maruts, the Ribhugans, consisting of three Ribhus are important characters of Ṛig-Veda. Ribhus are more subtle than Maruts.

Like Maruts, the Ribhus were not considered as God initially, but when their subtleties and merits became known, they were upgraded to the status of God.

The Ribhugans have eleven suktas in Ṛig-Veda. They are introduced in hymn 1.20.4 as one having the power to remove old age. The sukta 110 is of Ribhugans. In this sukta the Ribhugans are associated with immortality and power to restore youth to emaciated bodies. Their father is Sudhamva who was a descendent of Angiras. Rishis suggest that Ribhus are associated with brightness of light, as Angiras is associated with light. This sukta also means that God Twasta, who is chief artisan, carpenter of Gods and Guru of Ribhus, created the year, but

Ribhus as Gods of season divided the year into four parts or seasons. The sukta also indicates that dried earth (cow) gets refreshed by rainwater during the rainy season.

The sukta 1.161 is highly scientific. This sukta means that Ribhus are rays of the Sun. The hymn 7 speaks of cloning as the Ribhus made another horse from one horse. Hymn 12 indicates that even if Sun is not visible his rays are around and those who utilize the rays are prosperous. The sukta 14 is also scientific. To meet Ribhus, the Maruts move in the world of Gods, Agni moves on earth, Vayu in firmament and Varun in water streams. This hymn is very difficult to understand.

The sukta 60 of mandala three is also worth understanding. The reason due to which Ribhus achieved Godhood is stated in hymns 2. According to this hymn Ribhus made four seasons, provided earth with protective (fertile) cover and energized the horses of Indra. Since Indra appears to be personification of gravitational force, this hymn suggest that Ribhus are some kind of force that energizes or strengthens gravitational force. This needs further research.

The suktas 33, 34, 35, 36 and 37 of the fourth mandala are in praise of Ribhus and are highly informative. Ribhus are said to dwell in solar sphere. The radiation from the Sun is called Ribhus. The radiated rays of Sun have been divided in three categories and they are the three Ribhus as the three brothers. The eldest among the Ribhus is Ribhukshan, middle one is Baz and the youngest is Viswan. They are friendly with Indra and also Maruts, Aditya, Savita, mountains and rivulets.

The first Ribhu gives shapes to the radiated particles for nourishment of earth. The second Ribhus does scattering of the particles, properly shaped. The third makes the objects of nature strong and healthy.

Twasta is said to be a carpenter who designs the pole, erected at the place of Yagya. This pole means axis of the earth. It was vertical earlier but Ribhus tilted it and four seasons were created, Ribhus divided the sky in twelve parts and gave rains that increased fertility of soil and added rivulets and streams. The Ribhus created lands for agriculture. Ribhus made the two horses of Indra strong. The last hymn of this sukta 33 is much thought provoking "the Gods do not help without serious labor and pain." This message is for those who do not work hard but believe in getting everything by worshipping idols and by following rituals.

In Sukta 34, hymns 7 and 8 are very scientific. In hymn 8 oceans are said to be the giver of jewels. Hymn 9 indicates that the Aswins the forces at Dawn (Usha) are strengthened by solar radiations (Ribhus) that makes earth and sky younger and adds fertility to soil (cow) and made an armor around the earth (Ionosphere) to protect the earth. Griffith translated the armor as made for Gods. This Ionosphere is mentioned as sieve in hymn 9.97.56 given below.

eṣa viśvavit pavate manīṣī somo viśvasya bhuvanasya rājā |
drapsānīrayan vidatheṣvindurvi vāramavyaṃ samayāti yāti ||

(9.97.56)

In sukta 4.35 the occurrence of four seasons is repeatedly presented. Ribhus are said to be the giver of immortality.

The sukta 4.36 is very scientific. It says that the three-wheeled chariot of Aswins (sometimes drawn by mules which according to Griffith means the grey clouds of morning twilight), was constructed by Ribhus. The chariot is without horses and reins. The three wheels of Aswins are worth researching. It is also interpreted as processes of refining materials to filter their healthful properties, their distribution, and enhancement of those properties.

As per this sukta, the Ribhus give these qualities to Aswins. This means that health giving properties at dawn are due to solar radiations of special types.

The hymn 4 of this sukta refers to four seasons and bestowing the "cow with skin" which means enhancing the fertility of soil. It is for scholars of Agriculture to understand the Ribhus. Do the Ribhus help with nitrogen fixing in soil?

The cow (fertile soil) is well-explained in 8.101.15. Cow is the mother of Rudra, daughter of Vasus, sister of Adityas and source of nectar or Amrit. Here cow is not the animal as we commonly know.

mātā rudrāṇāṃ duhitā vasūnāṃ svasādityānāmamṛtasya nābhiḥ |
pra nu vocaṃ cikituṣe janāya mā ghāmanāghāmaditiṃ vadhiṣṭa ||
(8.101.15)

So who are the three Ribhus? Are they three types of photon? The physicists can opine.

Etasha

Etasha is an interesting character of Astronomy. He is presented as a Rishi who offered Som to Indra, and also as a competitor of the Sun in 1.61.15. He is one of the seven horses of the Sun.

Once Indra stopped the horses of the Sun then Etasha drew the wheel of Sun's chariot. Etasha caused the Sun to rise in the east. In a fight between the Sun and Etasha, Indra gave security to Etasha in the followin hymn 4.30.6.

yatrota martyāya kam ariṇā indra sūryam |
prāvaḥ śacībhir etaśam || (4.30.6)

ayaṃ cakram iṣaṇat sūryasya ny etaśaṃ rīramat sasṛmāṇam |
ā kṛṣṇa īṃ juhurāṇo jigharti tvaco budhne rajaso asya yonau ||
(4.7.14)

The above hymn, 4.17.14 is difficult to interpret. According to this hymn Indra urged the Sun to move and Etasha, who was going for war, had to return. This seems to suggest interaction between two stars represented by the Sun and Etasha. There appears to be fragmentation of the Sun. This suggests origin of planets out of fragments of the Sun drawn by Etasha's gravitation.

As per hymn 5.31.11, in the war between the Sun and Etasha, Indra took away one wheel of the Sun's chariot and used it to kill the enemies.

Hymn 5.29.5 presents Etasha as an energy linked with the Sun's rays.

yat tudat sūra etaśaṃ vaṅkū vātasya parṇinā |
vahat kutsamārjuneyaṃ śatakratuḥ tsarad ghandharvamastṛtam ||
(8.1.11)

Hymn 8.1.11 refers to atomic sub-particles. Indra keeps them together and withholds fragmentation by the Sun's rays. Here Indra takes help of Kutsa who resembles Indra, which suggests that formulae for gravitational force and electrical force are similar. This hymn is for physicists.

Vayu

Vayu is another very important mystical and scientific character of Ṛig-Veda. Vayu means wind and so this God Vayu in the ordinary sense means wind. But it is different from Maruts who are storm Gods associated with hurricane, blizzards, or tornado.

Vayu is very subtle. He is the soul of all the Gods. From the breath of the Absolute God has born Vayu. He gives health, longevity and unlimited strength. Vayu lives in Antariksha. His movement is not straight but oblique. He is the fastest among all Gods. Sometimes Vayu is associated with Indra. Vayu is born after Agni as indicated in hymn 1.31.3. Per hymn 1.60.1 Agni was made a friend of Bhrigu (Sun's ray) by Vayu.

vahniṃ yaśasaṃ vidathasya ketuṃ suprāvyaṃ dūtaṃ sadyoartham |
dvijanmānaṃ rayimiva praśastaṃ rātiṃ bharad bhṛghavemātariśvā ||
(1.60.1)

Sukta 134 of first mandala gives a good description of Vayu. He is as good a Som drinker as Indra. His chariot has two red horses. This can be compared with the horses of Indra's chariots. The Vayu is presented in hymn 4 as commonly known wind which is active in providing rain. In hymn 6, Vayu is giver of Pran Vayu, life-giving air.

Agni appeared in high Antariksha (1.143.2). It is to be noted that Rishi Matrisha brought Agni from heaven and gave it to Bhrigu (Sun's rays). In sukta 187, which is in praise of grains personified as Gods, Vayu appears in the fifth hymn but it is undercover. In this hymn the word Trita appears which means combination of Indra, Vayu and Marut.

In hymn 3.49.4, Vayu is presented as the chariot of Indra. As per 3.56.8, the inhabitants of the three best places are Agni (in the world of no decay); Vayu (in the best world); and Surya (in the world of intense brightness).

triruttamā dūṇaśā rocanāni trayo rājantyasurasya vīrāḥ |
ṛtāvāna iṣirā dūḷabhāsastrirā divo vidathe santu devāḥ || (3.56.8)

The sukta 57 of mandala 4 is in praise of God Kshetrapati and others connected with agriculture. This sukta indicates the large and simple hearts of Rishis who considered agriculture, and grains or anything beneficial for humans, plants and this earth as God. Kshetrapati is agriculture personified and is being treated as friend of all. Some think that Kshetrapati means either Rudra or Agni.

Vayu appears in the hymn 5 of sukta 57 mandala 4. Here two Gods are Shuna and Saur. This duo is respectively considered as Indra and Vayu or Vayu and Aditya. Professor Grossman interprets these two as plough and plough man. In hymn 8 also Vayu and Surya appear. This shows that these two are closely connected with agriculture. In 7.33.3 three Gods, Agni, Vayu, and Surya are mentioned who fertilize the earth.

even nu kaṃ sindhumebhistatāreven nu kaṃ bhedamebhirjaghāna |
even nu kaṃ dāśarājñe sudāsaṃ prāvadindro brahmaṇā vo
vasiṣṭhāḥ || (7.33.3)

Agni produces a fertilizing fluid on earth, Vayu in air, and Surya (Sun) in sky. The three persons noble in nature are Vasu, Rudra and Aditya. In depth, all of them are the same.

pra vāvṛje suprayā barhireṣāmā viśpatīva bīriṭa iyāte |
viśāmaktoruṣasaḥ pūrvahūtau vāyuḥ pūṣā svastaye niyutvān ||
(7.39.2)

As per the above hymn (7.39.2), Vayu and Pusan arrive between the end of night and the arrival of dawn (Usha) upon a call for the benefit of all living beings. This period is Brahma Bela and here calling of Vayu means Pranayan or a process of controlled breathing. Pranayan is said to regulate Pran Vayu which is the Vayu that sustains life. In hymn 7.91.3, Vayu's complexion is described as fair. In 8.7.24 the word Trita is mentioned which means Indra, Vayu and Marut, as stated earlier. In 8.26.20 it is mentioned that Vayu is the son-in-law of Twasta married to Saranyu, the daughter of Twasta. Elsewwhere it is mentioned that Saranyu was wife of Vivasawan and not Vayu.

yo aśvebhirvahate vasta usrāstriḥ sapta saptatīnām |
ebhiḥ somebhiḥ somasudbhiḥ somapā dānāya śukrapūtapāḥ | |
(8.46.26)

The above hymn suggests that Vayu, drinker of Som and increaser of strength travels on his two horses and gives protection to 3x7x70 = 1470 cows. It is not clear as to what is meant by 1470 cows. This is for research.

Saraswati

Goddess Saraswati appears in the third sukta of the first mandala (1.3.10,11 and 12).

pāvakā naḥ sarasvatī vājebhirvājinīvatī |
yajñaṃ vaṣṭu dhiyāvasuḥ ||
codayitrī sūnṛtānāṃ cetantī sumatīnām |
yajñaṃ dadhe sarasvatī ||
maho arṇaḥ sarasvatī pra cetayati ketunā |
dhiyo viśvā vi rājati ||

At the very beginning of Veda, Rishi Madhurchanda Viswamitra says that "She (Saraswati) provides inspiration for sacrifice. She awakens good intellect."

In Ṛig-Veda Goddess Saraswati is mentioned fifty-two times. She is Goddess of eloquence and sacred poetry. But her most important role is inspiration.

She is represented as the wife of Brahma. The meaning of Saraswati is "flowing like river, inspiration". She is clad in white spotless saree and her vehicle is white crane (Hansa). She has a musical instrument (Veena) in her hand. Saraswati is associated with Goddesses Ila, and Bharati or Mahi. They mean "flowing inspiration", "vastness with intense bright light", and "vision of knowledge" respectively. They are introduced below.

Ila

Goddess Ila first appears in hymn 1.13.9. Ila is also the wife of Buddha (Mercury) who controls intellect of humans, as per astrology. Buddha is the son of Moon and Tara.

iḷā sarasvatī mahī tisro devīrmayobhuvaḥ |
barhiḥ sīdantvasridhaḥ || (1.13.9)

She appears twelve times in Ṛig-Veda. She is said to be the Goddess of sacred speech and action. She is also said to be butter and ghee (clarified butter) of cow's milk. She is also considered a Revelation, which is one of the faculties of intuitive reasoning. She is also said to be Dristi which means vision of knowledge of truth.

From these brief introductions it is clear that she is the essence of light (cows), a very subtle meaning which can be understood by enlightened persons.

Bharati

She appears fourteen times in Ṛig-Veda. Her first appearance is in hymn 1.13.9 along with Ila but her name as Mahi is said to be identical with Bharati who is Goddess of speech and is associated with Saraswati same as Ila. Mahi is full of cows (illumination) and so is Bharati.

The root of word Bharati is "Bha" (Sanskrit) which means very intense light and light could represent knowledge. And this root word explains the meaning of "India that is Bharat". Bharat means absorbed in intense light which means absorbed in knowledge.

These subtle conceptions of inspiration, revelations, and knowledge by Rishis gradually started disappearing as Ila, and Bharati (Mahi) were merged into Saraswati who turned into an idol.

Urvashi

Urvashi is a celestial nymph, Apsara of Chandra lok (world of Moon).

The word Apsara means born out of Ap which is generally understood as water. Ap is defined in the tenth mandala. Ap, Som, and Jal existed before Indra was born.

Urvashi, a nymph, however, gained the status of a Goddess in sukta 95 of the tenth mandala, which describes her love affair with Pururva. In Madbahgawat, this story is detailed in the fourteenth chapter. Pururva and Urvashi had a son, Ayus, who established the Chandravanshi (belonging to Moon) clan among Kshatriyas. The other clan being Suryavanshi (belonging to Sun).

If de-personified, Urvashi means morning mist around ponds, lakes, and rivers. Pururva saw her near a pond. Pururwa means the rising Sun of early morning who is very pleasant and handsome. When Pururwa comes Urvashi deserts him, which means that with the arrival of the Sun, mists disappear.

The root of Urvashi word is Ur which means heart and womb. Vashi means control. So Urvashi means a women whose womb is within her control which means that she will conceive and deliver child only at her desire.

It appears that Urvashi is not a nymph nor a woman. The expression "Court dancer of world of Moon" refers to the mist around lakes or ponds governed by forces or rays of the Moon. The beauty of mist was personified as a woman, an Apsara (a nymph). Similarly, there are other nymphs of Indralok (world of Indra). Indra also means Sun.

Rati

The word Rati means love. Rati is personified as a woman and is given the status of a Goddess. She is wife of Kamdeo, the most handsome and Lord of sex. (Please see Appendix D about Kamdeo).

The Goddess of sukta 1.179 is Rati. This sukta suggests proper age difference between husband and wife for good offsprings. It is about a conversation between Rishi Agastya and his wife Lopmudra. Their age difference was too much. Agastya was much older. The young Lopmudra desired for love and children. She says that old age weakens the body, so for good offspring the husband has to be young and strong.

This sukta (179) is very interesting and gives many messages.

i) There must be proper age difference between young male and female and both should have good health for good children.

ii) Sex should be with the intention of having good children and not for enjoyment. This applies even to those who are practicing Brahmacharya (celibacy).

Raka

She is the Goddess who governs the full-moon night. She appears in Ṛig-Veda hymns 2.32.4, and 5. She gives good intellect, healthy offsprings and abundant grains. She is also associated with child birth. Raka is associated with another lunar Goddess, Sinivali who aids birth of children. She is sister of Gods (2.32.6). She is associated with Saraswati (10.184.2) and Aswini for good child birth. As per this hymn, there is protection by Sinivali, help in conception by Saraswati and stability by Aswini. Two more Goddesses- Kuhan or Gungu and Anumati, not mentioned in Ṛig-Veda are also associated with Raka and Sinivali. Gynecologists can interpret these Goddesses.

Ratri

Ratri means night. She is also a Goddess, sister of Usha (dawn). Ratri appears in 1.35.1.

hvayāmy aghnim prathamaṃ svastaye hvayāmi mitrāvaruṇāv ihāvase |
hvayāmi rātrīṃ jaghato niveśanīṃ hvayāmi devaṃ savitāram ūtaye ||

All the stars of the constellation in the sky are her eyes to the entire universe. She offers all types of glamour and rest (10.127.1). She is sister of Usha (1.13.27, 1.142.7) and both (Rati and Usha) together are called Ushasankta.

Both are daughters of Dyulok, which means world of light (7.2.5). Both are maidens having high prosperity (2.31.5). Even though both Ratri and Usha have different complexions, they are always together, they move together, never stay at one place (1.113.3, 1.142.7). If one thinks over hymns, one will salute the Rishis who told the geographical fact of day and nigh (rotation of the earth) in melodious songs with beautiful words.

Usha

Usha, the inseparable sister of Ratri, is the most beautiful, kind, generous and loved by all Gods as well as humans. She can be realized only by those who look at her. Usha's beauty and charm can not be expressed in simple words.

The importance of this Goddess Usha, can be understood from the fact that there are twenty suktas for her in Ṛig-Veda. She has been mentioned three hundred times whereas Surya (Sun), is mentioned only one hundred fifty one times.

bhaghasya svasā varuṇasya jāmiruṣaḥ sūnṛte prathamā jarasva |
paścā sa daghyā yo aghasya dhātā jayema taṃ dakṣiṇayā rathena ||
(1.123.5)

Usha is said to be sister of Varun and Bhag (Sun). She is born in the world of light, she is said to be the daughter of Surya but also she is said to be the wife of Surya. In another context, she is also said to be the wife of Aswins. She is also closely connected with Moon, Indra and Brihaspati.

All these relations and associations portray the qualities of Usha, the dawn. To those who see and realize her daily in the early morning hours, Usha gives intellect and good thoughts (Brihaspati), good health (Aswins), good physical strength (Indra), good mind and peace (Moon) and good vitality (Sun). She gets up before the Sun, so she is said to be the wife of Sun. She has her qualities derived from the Sun, so she is also said to be the daughter of the Sun.

Usha appears in 1.30.20 and 22. The Rishi says that Usha's qualities are so vast that one cannot enjoy it all. Usha comes with horses (Ashwa) which means with light rays and rays of various hues and color. She is daughter of Dyulok (the world of light), in the vicinity of the Sun or perhaps the Rishis meant the galaxy.

aghne vivasvaduṣasaścitraṃ rādho amartya |
ā dāśuṣe jātavedo vahā tvamadyā devānuṣarbudhaḥ || (1.44.1)

As per hymn 1.44.1, special forces become active at dawn. So it is said that many Gods are awake at dawn. Here it is again pointed out that Gods are not like human beings, but are various forces, or energies of nature. God or Devta in Sanskrit, means one who gives for betterment of lives. At dawn nature offers all sorts of qualities for good survival.

The sukta 92 of first mandala is by Rishi Gautama Rahugan who belongs to the family of Gautama Rishi. Gautama, a Sanskrit word, means the best fast walker. Moon, who moves fast, is also said to be Gautama. In this sukta (92) the Rishi has described Usha in a very enchanting manner. As per the Rishi, Usha is like a dancer who with her different forms enchants all. Usha, like a cow exposes her udders to give a flow of healthy streams of milk for all. Here it is again emphasized that cow means light and milk means radiance and other health-giving benefits of light. The Rishi also compares Usha with a beautiful lady, well-dressed and with jewels, smiling to please her husband.

Husband represents a person in deep thoughts and meditation to realize any activity of the nature. A man who is dedicated to understanding Usha, her radiances, and her health-giving properties can claim to be her husband. In real life also, such is the relationship between a husband and wife who are together enjoying a happy married life, dedicated to each other. It is the inner light that makes realization of each other possible.

The Rishi also indicated that Usha makes one younger every day. Perhaps it hints at the anti-aging benefits of Usha.

Usha is said to be mother of cows (illumination or light) and is a form of Aditi, the supreme mother of cows, visible light as well as cosmic rays. Rishi Kutsa Angiras has said so in sukta 113 of the first mandala. In this mandala, the joint movement of night and dawn clearly means rotation of the earth on its axis. The Rishi also compares Usha with a beautiful young girl in a shining milky white dress.

As per 10.3.3 Usha is Agni's sister and as per 8.60.9 Agni is the lord of all energies. All energies are combined and personified as Agni. It means that Usha comes with various types of energies.

As per 1.116.17, Usha is Sun's daughter and wins a horse race and comes to the chariot of Aswins where the three (two Aswins and Usha) look very beautiful.

As per 1.123.8 and 6.59.6 Usha travels thirty Yogan (a Yogan is Vedic standard for length measurement) each day or steps. Griffith translates thirty steps as Aryan's division of day and night each step being equal to two Dands (48 minutes) for length measurement of each day.

The description of Usha in 1.129.10 and 11 appears highly sensuous. She is compared with a young women going to her husband Sun and returning with shining face and exposing her illuminated breast and showing all her limbs. A scholar of literature can explain.

As per 3.17.3 there are three types of Usha, called Ekah, Aheen, and Satra and these three are the mothers of Agni. The sukta 75 of seventh mandala is full of nature, beauty of Usha and prayer for enlightenment, strength and good children.

In the sukta 65 of the sixth mandala, Usha is said to be worth seeing on mountain tops. Because of her, the Angiras (flame of Sun) released the cows (Sun's rays). It means that Sun's rays appear after Usha.

In sukta 80 of the seventh mandala Usha is giver of horses (force) and cows (light) and increases milk and clarified butter.

There is an interesting event concerning Usha. Her chariot was broken by Indra. This event is found in hymns 2.15.6, 4.30.8, 10.73.6 and 10.138.5. As Indra also means Sun, so with the Sun's arrival Usha vanishes at a particular place of observation. The chariot of Usha is said to be broken but hymn 10.138.5 makes clear that with arrival of the Sun, Goddess Usha moves her chariot ahead. This also indicates rotation of the earth. Griffith's translation that Usha leaves her chariot and went upon her way is not accurate. If Griffith's translation is accepted then it means that Usha moves ahead with her glamour, beauty and charm and leaves the early sun rays behind.

The hymn 8.24.30 is highly spiritual as well as scientific. In this hymn, Usha is said to be destroyer of Maya. If someone asks of Usha as to where does king Waru live, then she has to tell that the killer of enemies, Waru, lives near river Gomati. In translation by Griffith, the name is not Waru, but Vala. The name Vala appears in 1.11.5 and also 10.68.9. Vala is brother of Vritra killed by Indra. Vala steals cows of Gods and keeps them in a cave which is full of treasures. The word Vala signifies enclosure or circumscription. Vala is said to be enclosure of the radiances. So Vala is not darkness but he causes darkness. He is killed by Brihaspati and broken into fragments.

If the above characters Vala and Vritra are de-personified then some astronomical events may be explained. Like black hole, Vritra conceals light and everything. Vala also appears to be some phenomenon that causes darkness. It would be debatable as to whether Vala means black spots of the sun (sun spots) or black holes.

As per the second line of the hymn Vala lives near the river Gomati. On this river bank is the city of Lucknow (in India). Griffith's view is that a river, affluent of Indus (Sindhu) was named as Gomati or Gumati. The present Gomati falls into the river Ganges, but what is the meaning of the word Gomati? "Go" means illumination and "Mati" means mind, intellect. So Gomati means illuminated mind. Vala was killed by Brihaspati who is God of illuminated intellect, so the whole story means that when the mind is illuminated the darkness of ignorance vanishes. Griffith considers Usha as an Aurora, the astronomical phenomenon.

The relationship of Usha with various Gods must be understood. She is wife of the Sun because Sun chases her like an extremely attached husband. Usha is called daughter of the Sun, because she rises when the Sun approaches. This is how the wife and daughter relationship has been explained by scholar Muir, as quoted by Griffith.

Usha is also associated with Goddesses Dakshina and Sarma. She is sister of Agni and is attached with Aswins. She is also close to Indra and Brihaspati. This means attached with energy, health, healthy organs of senses and intellect.

Scholars of science can explain various forces and energies of nature which appear with Usha. The most important is the health-giving benefits of the early morning sun's rays. Rising Sun is called Savita. The hour prior to sunrise is called Brahma Bela meaning Brahma's hour. The rising Sun, Savita or Bhag improves eyesight and tones up heart and mind. This period of Usha is for growth and expansion of energy, intellect and all that is good for human health so this hour is Brahma bela. Brahma also means expansion.

Dakshina

It is said that Dakshina Goddess is a female form of the God Daksha. She is identified with Usha, the Goddess of Dawn who brings light and energy. As Daksha means mental power of judgment and discernment, so is Dakshina. She appears in hymn 1.18.5 with God Som, Indra and Brihaspati, who is Lord of total knowledge.

Hymn 1.123.1 appears to be in praise of Usha but scholars like Wilson interprets it to be in praise of Dakshina.

The hymn 2.11.21, however, indicates that Dakshina means honorarium or salary that a person desiring Yagya gives to the priests.

The hymn 3.58.1 is again interesting. This hymn is in praise of Aswins and the Goddess appearing in this hymn is Dakshina and not Usha according to Griffith. He also indicates that Dakshina's son is Agni, the Sun.

In the land of Ṛig-Veda, Dakshina is known only as the honorarium or salary that a priest gets or demands from the person on whose desire the Yagya has been performed. Some priests consider Dakshina as a matter of right. So is the case with Gurus (masters) who get Guru Dakshina from disciples (Shishya) and Guru may demand according to his desire.

Here it is notable that Guru is treated as greater than God. Guru gives pleasure and enlightenment by eliminating ignorance from the mind of a disciple. In Sanskrit "Guru" means one who removes darkness or ignorance.

Sarma

Sarma is a she wolf in the service of Gods like Brihaspati. She is the Goddess and is intuition personified. Veterinarians can perhaps understand why a she wolf has been selected to represent intuition.

In 1.52.3 Sarma appears with Indra and Angiras.

In this hymn she is associated with her sons. She is said to be mother of two sons each are four-eyed and are the watch dogs of Yama, the God of death. Hymn 1.72.8 suggests that Sarma has found the cattle (cows) hidden by demons.

vidad yadī saramā rughṇamadrermahi pāthaḥ pūrvyaṃ sadhryak kaḥ |
aghraṃ nayat supadyakṣarāṇāmachā ravaṃ prathamā jānatī ghāt ||
(3.31.6)

The above hymn indicates that in darkness Sarma, the "light footed", made a path, through the mountains and liberated the cows. Hymn 4.16.8 indicates that Sarma is with Indra and Angiras while liberating the cows (light).

In hymns 7.55.2, 3, and 4 Sarma's sons have been mentioned. In 7.55.2 Sarma's sons appear to be of yellow color with projected teeth. In hymn 7.55.3 they are advised not to bark at the worshippers of Indra. In 7.55.4 a wild boar terrifies Sarma's sons. The Rishis request Sarma's sons to go to sleep.

As mentioned earlier, the sons of Sarma are the watch dogs of Yama, the God of death. The Rishi advises them to sleep. It means disease and old age should not terrify any one and one should sleep peacefully. The Rishi indicates that Yama should not come in the house. In this sukta the struggle between good health and disease is referred to.

This complete suktas (55) of the seventh mandala is amusing and mysterious. The God is Vastopati. The word Vasto means architecture. Vastopati is said to be the God of house. He is praised for beautiful and comfortable architectural design to ensure comfort and prosperity of a household. The God Vastopati has appeared only four times in Ṛig-Veda. According to Griffith, Vastopati is Moon God. Griffith thinks that the hymns of this sukta (55) are unconnected. This is not acceptable.

In 10.14.10 appears the word "Sarmeya" which is translated by Griffith as sons of Sarma. But this Sanskrit word Sarmeya also means co-traveler. The Sarmeyas are four-eyed. In the context of Mahabharata these two Sarmeyas represent old age and disease but the meaning of four-eyed is not clear. To avoid disease certain organs, such as brain, heart, stomach and kidney must be healthy. Perhaps these four organs are represented by the four eyes of Sarmeya.

Sukta 108 of the 10th mandala deals with conversation between Sarma and Pani. This sukta is of political, spiritual and scientific significance. Sarma goes to Pani as Ambassador of Indra and asks Pani to release the cows stolen by him and kept in the cave. Pani expresses surprise as to how she reached this place. Sarma tells Pani that Indra is invincible so one should not fight with Indra. She also warns Pani that Brihaspati may torture him if cows are not returned. Pani wants to bribe Sarma and offers her some of the stolen cows and wishes to treat her as sister. Sarma understands this diplomacy and refuses all offers. She threatens Pani that Brihaspati, Moon, and Rishis have known about the stolen cows.

The meaning of Pani and Sarma need to be understood. From the root "Pan" Pani means a person involved in worldly affairs. Such persons are also called Asura. Such persons are absorbed with self-defense and are selfish. Their selfishness and involvement with worldly pleasures clouds enlightenment (cows are concealed in cave). Sarma is the inner mind in quest of truth. Sarma ultimately recovers the cows (enlightenment).

If Sarma and Pani are de-personified then scholars of physics have to look to the subtleties. The paragraph below is worth understanding.

The first hymn of this sukta 108 of the 10th mandala has word Rasa in it which is said to represent a stream of air around the earth at high altitude. Pani asks Sarma has to how she crossed the river Rasa?

kimichantī saramā predamānaḍ dūre hyadhvā jaghuriḥparācaiḥ |
kāsmehitiḥ kā paritakmyāsīt kathaṃ rasāyāatarah payāṃsi ||

(10.108.1)

Griffith has explained the meaning of Rasa after quoting other scholars like Max Muller. According to him, Rasa is a river which is the changed name of Ranha, a river known to the Zoroastrians. The Rishis used this word for a stream of air at high altitude above the earth. This stream of air is probably the one detected by jet pilots at high altitude during the Korean war and is now known as the Jet Stream. This word Rasa also appears in hymn 1.112.12.

yābhī rasāṃ kṣodasodnaḥ pipinvathuranaśvaṃ yābhī
rathamāvataṃ jiṣe |
yābhistriśoka usriyā udājata tābhir... || (1.112.12)

According to the above hymn chariots without horses were carried to the destination by Rasa. This Rasa, glorified as a Goddess, also appears in 5.41.15, and 5.53.9. Thus the Rishis had the knowledge of existence of this river of air at high altitude above the earth.

Pani asks Sarma as to how this river was crossed. It means that Sarma (nature's property, force, energy or rays) travels between the earth and its upper atmosphere. As Indra and Brihaspati are also involved, it seems that gravity has relations with Sarma.

Some interpret Sarma as Usha who liberates light from darkness represented by Pani. Both Sarma and Pani are subjects of research.

"The Sanskrit work for creation is Srishti, Projection. What is meant by 'God created things out of nothing'? The universe is projected out of God. He becomes the universe and it all returns to Him, and again it proceeds forth, and again returns. Through all eternity it will go on in that way."

– Swami Vivekananda

Creation

The study of Ṛig-Veda will remain incomplete if one does not try to understand the creation of this universe.

The five suktas - 81, 82, 129, 130, and 190, of the tenth mandala are about creation of the universe. Rishis have posed such questions as a common man could ask. Who is the creator? Where was He standing while He was creating this universe? Where was the creator living when this universe did not exist? From where did the creator obtain the materials to create the galaxies and the earth? What was the material of which he created this universe?

The questions have been posed by Rishi Vishwakarma Vauvan. He is considered a Twasta—a well-known artisan who works for Gods. This Rishi's daughter was Surenu who was later named Sangya and was married to Vivaswavan.

The Rishis give answers of the questions.

> "Without any place, to stand upon, He - the unique creator - has His eyes, mouth, arms and foot all around and He is the manager of His creation."
>
> "He, the creator, had held the basic element (Ap) in which all Gods live. In the navel of this creator, who is not born, exists the ultimate element due to which the entire universe is stable."

> "You humans do not know about the creator who made this universe. The creator is aloof from His creations but also He lives inside all matters created by Him. Ignorant persons, busy in discussion about Him and busy with personal nourishment and life, unnecessarily discuss about the creator. Such persons do not visualize or realize Him—the Creator."

Science scholars can think about the meaning of Rishi's observation. "He is away and different from His creation but also He exists in each of His creation."

Similar questions are in sukta 129.

> "There was neither 'non-existent' nor 'existent'. There was no earth, sky or anything above it and there was no universe which covers all. Was water there - unfathomable depth of water?"
>
> "There was no death and immortality did not exist. There was no idea of day and night. There was no air to breathe. Only one existed - the Brahma, and nothing else."
>
> "Before creation there was darkness of ignorance. Everything was covered by untruth."
>
> "At first, Paramatma had a desire for creation, the desire being the primal seed and germ of spirit. Sages searched in their hearts and discovered the existent's kinship in the non-existent."
>
> "The rays of the Gods, having capabilities for creation, 'obliquely' moved upward and downward and rays got scattered. The Gods activated 'Jal'—the world of action below and the world of energy above."

At the end of this sukta the Rishi boldly accepts limitations of his imagination and realizations in his mind and heart.

> "Who knows and who can declare from where creation started and how it started? Scholars were born after this creation so who is capable to say about beginning of this creation."

The last hymn is much interesting.

> "From where did this creation start? Who created, who did not create? This is known to only He - Parameshwar, the ultimate God. Only He is the chairman. Quite possibly He also may not be knowing details about His creation."

This entire sukta is for imagination, and realization of knowledge of science and spiritual approach.

One may like to have clues to understand this sukta.

> "Non-existent does not actually exist but has in itself certain latent condition which, due to the absence of distinctiveness, was not an 'entity'; at the same time, being the instrument of the world (creation), it was not a 'non-entity'."

Many Rishis have expressed their eagerness to know about the creator.

In hymn 1.164.6 the Rishi asks about the unborn He, about His looks and appearance. He who created the "six worlds" and made them stable. The Rishi admits his ignorance about Him and asks sages for knowledge about Him.

acikitvāñcikituṣaścidatra kavīn pṛchāmi vidmane na vidvān |
vi yastastambha ṣaḷ imā rajāṃsyajasya rūpe kimapi svidekam ||

In the hymn 46 of this sukta, the Rishis say that all Gods are from Him and all Gods are His various manifestations. This is unified field theory's predecessor.

The sukta 146 asks as to what is meant by "six worlds".

In this sukta 129 of the tenth mandala the two worlds indicate duality in unity.

According to Griffith many have tried to explain this sukta. Professor Whitney has expressed his view in the journal of the American Oriental Society. Max Muller has also translated the sukta (129) of the tenth mandala.

The sukta 130 is practical, scientific and neither sentimental nor spiritual unlike the previous sukta 129. The Rishi says-

> "This creation is full of actions and the fabric made of the 'five elements' are woven. Good as well as bad materials or fabrics are by predecessors."
>
> "Parameshwar, the Almighty, is the creator and destroyer. He expands this creation. His rays are at the place of actions and His rays create bliss and happiness." Hereafter, the Rishis hints at the various types of waves and their association with Gods.

Again, the Rishi questions-

> "What was the extent of the actions by all forces of God and what were the Gods resolutions? What was the effect of the actions? What were the Chhandas (metres)?" The Rishi says that the seven divine Rishis, God-like, were versed in metres and rules of actions (rituals) and their "path are to be followed."

These seven Rishis are Bharadwaj, Kashyap, Gautama, Atri, Vashistha, Vishwamitra, and Jamadagni.

The theme of this sukta is sound waves emanating from different metres of hymns. These waves increase intellect, mental and physical strengths. Scholars of music in association with scholars of physics and medical science can interpret the metres such as Gayatri, Tristy, and Jagti

The sukta 190 of the tenth mandala is also related to Rishis views about creations. This sukta has only three hymns, but this sukta is said to be the best sukta of Ṛig-Veda for 'purity and prosperity'. This sukta deals with Time, its origin and its manifestations. It is a highly scientific sukta. The God of this sukta is Bhav Vrita. It means the "wheel that happened". This wheel represents the macroscopic scale of "Time" of creation and deluge (destruction). This "Time", is analogous to Day and Night. Day represents the time when the universe existed and the night represents the period when the universe did not exist.

The hymns are as follows:

ṛtaṃ ca satyaṃ cābhīddhāt tapaso.adhyajāyata |
tatorātryajāyata tataḥ samudro arṇavaḥ ||
samudrādarṇavādadhi saṃvatsaro ajāyata |
ahorātrāṇividadhad viśvasya miṣato vaśī ||
sūryācandramasau dhātā yathāpūrvamakalpayat |
divaṃ capṛthivīṃ cāntarikṣamatho svaḥ ||

This sukta means the ingredients of creation of this universe comes from Him and during the period of non existence or destruction (deluge), of this universe its ingredients are absorbed by Him. According to Griffith:

> "From fervor kindled to its height Eternal Law and Truth were born. Then the Night was produced and then the billowy flood of sea arose." From enormous light's heat came the eternal materials and also visible materials of nature.

Does it suggest the Big-bang theory of creation?

> "When flow started on the ocean of elementary materials, came the concept of 'Time' and also time itself."

Perhaps the Rishis theory of time is that movement or flow is time. In static state there is no time.

> "The ultimate Day and Night (creation and destruction) is within His time of one blink of eyes."

This may be interpreted as an explosion of duration measuring billionth of a second which caused creation. The Rishi compares this duration with "blink of His eyes." The Rishis had calculated and established a scale of time. In this context Appendix-K may be seen.

He, the Almighty, is busy in His job of creation, maintenance and destruction. Nothing has been made permanent by Him. Lord Krishna also says in Gita that even though He may sit idle, all the agencies created by Him are doing their jobs. He is automation expert in the modern sense but He is always keeping His eyes on all the instruments. If any aspect of it goes wrong, He corrects. This has been said by Lord Krishna that "whenever right is subdued and wrong starts ruling, He appears and corrects." Those who believe in the divine power will accept this theory of creation—there is no doubt. What is needed is a collective effort to understand the scientific concepts underlying these suktas and hymns.

Conclusion

Our effort to comment on Ṛig-Veda and on the knowledge of science and technology lying within the Vedic Mantras may be considered by many, especially by the believers in rituals, as highly presumptuous. But it would be extreme disrespect to the Rishis, our predecessors, if one does not try to understand what the Rishis have said.

Rishis had known the various truths about the Nature, one of them being—"whatever is inside human body is outside the body." They, however, did not say that whatever is outside the body is inside the body also. The Rishis were aware of the large reservoir of Nature's capacities, various energies and forces and they utilized those capacities. For example, long distance communication of words through sound waves of low frequency. Scientists are still trying to understand the methods of communication in the world of animals. There is a glimpse of the supernatural powers of Rishis, called Munis in sukta 10.136. The Rishis' thoughts were forces and they controlled diseases through the power of their thoughts. The hymn 15 of sukta 136 of the tenth mandala is for restoring a sick person to health.

Swami Vivekananda has explained about restoration of good health. The cells of a healthy body are arranged in a particular manner. When disease enters a body the arrangements of cells are disturbed. By proper diet, lifestyle and meditation the cells can be restored to their original healthy state. Thus without medicine, many diseases can be controlled or cured. In a way, this explanation pertains to psycho-somatic theory of diseases.

The Rishis utilized the sound waves of hymns for various purposes. As an organ, ear has a vital role for both humans and animals. Hearing is said to be more effective than seeing. Lullaby, mother's melodious songs, are enjoyed by children. A child, even in mother's womb, is affected by whatever the mother hears with concentration.

The Rishis considered 'knowledge' a God. This shows their understanding about Gods. Not idols, not human-like, but abstract. The sukta 71 of the tenth mandala—of which the God is knowledge, deals with elementary to the highest knowledge stated as Brahma Gyan. The Vedas are said to be the means to reach the highest knowledge, which is divine and scientific.

In this sukta the Rishis has very clearly said that those who are not associated with men of knowledge, those who do not take pains to know pure knowledge, they make a mess of words. There is a proverb in Sanskrit meaning that cobwebs of words are denser than dense forests where mind wanders like a wild animal.

About Gods, it has been very clearly said that all are one and their source is one. The sukta 55 of the third mandala is about unity of all Gods. This sukta has 22 mantras (hymns), all indicating this unity. In spite of such clear messages from Rishis, their descendents quarrel over importance of various Gods.

Non-believers in books of Veda may have various questions. For example, they may critique that the Ṛig-Veda appears as Geocentric and not Heliocentric. The Geocentric belief is wrong.

But Yajur-Veda, the offshoot of Ṛig-Veda is very clear that this globe (earth) along with water revolves around the Sun. Yajur-Veda also says that the "Sun moves on its circumference and not around any object." These have been quoted in the book Satyarth Prakash by Swami Dyanand Saraswati. According to him, Ṛig-Veda hymn 10.65.6 means, "earth, known as 'cow' revolves around the Sun." Griffith's translation is translucent, as he says "Cow, yielding milk, goes her appointed way."

The trouble with progeny of the Rishis is that they overlooked the intricate matters of science which are being discovered by modern science now. Vedic hymns have at least five dimensions, namely—literature, spiritualism, science, music and effects of music on animate and inanimate objects. The progeny of the Rishi's thought that the Rishis spoke about spiritualism only. They did not understand the complete message and devoted themselves to idolatry, superstition, and meaningless rituals. Again the example of word "cow" (gau) may be taken. According to Veda, "cow" means earth, light, sun-rays, or speech not just the animal. The progeny of Rishis instead of understanding the real meaning of cow and taking advantage of its benefits such as the solar energy, fought wars for protection of cows.

In the land of Veda, there is deep rooted caste system. This is also based on wrong interpretation of the hymns of Ṛig-Veda.

People have misinterpreted the Varna system of social hierarchy where caste was defined by ones' action and not by birth. People do not know that the meaning of "Shudra" is ignorant. A person can be Shudra (by action) if one is ignorant of the manners of living, irrespective of one's birth.

Rishis did not discriminate between men and women. Among the Rishis of the Vedic period there were several women as is evident by the hymns of the Vedas. Simialrly, Rishis did not discriminate between a son and a daughter. They even desired for a daughter.

Another point to consider is that when the Gods are various forces or energies and elements of nature are personified then with whom did the great saints and prophets like Ramakrishna, or Moses talk? Did they talk with vacant space? This sukta 10.71 indicated various types of waves at various frequency existing in environment. If a person is to tune oneself to a specific frequency he or she can attain a knowledge not known to masses in general.

It can be understood that waves emanating from an individual body are "concentrated", which subsequently mix with different types of waves or radiations existing in the nature. The waves from a human body selectively absorb nature's waves which in turn are analyzed by brain as feelings of light, sound, smell, touch or taste. This phenomenon may be considered as communication with God. The living body works as a highly developed Radar, functioning as transmitter and receiver both. The capacity of brain is enormous which no human can understand. This enormity of brain is a minute reflection of the part of the Infinite, existing in everybody, known as soul or Atma (in Sanskrit).

Perhaps physicists can reply to such queries by explaining various types of waves or vibrations emanating from every living being, human, animals, plants and even elements like radio-active materials and reflected by inanimate objects.

We have read "Raman's effect" about scattering of light. Such scatterings of various types are going on in the vast and unseen space about which Rishis have sung various hymns. This cannot be seen, but felt by elevated minds. Persons in search of truth feel and try to understand those waves and they are the Rishis, like Einstein, Newton, J.C.Bose, and Chandrashekhar. Many had seen apples falling from a tree but it was Newton who saw gravitation force in the fall of an apple. He was a Rishi in search of truth.

It appears that the progeny of Rishis got themselves entangled in the cobweb of wrong interpretation of Vedas and absolute ignorance of science in the Vedas.

Rishis knew the truth about Gods. They were for following the wishes and commands of the Almighty which are beyond time or space, races or religions, which are for benefits of all. The Rishis listened to His wishes, discussed among themselves and recorded the truth in hymns.

Let this spirit of truth come to all, especially to the custodians of the Vedas and its literatures, so that darkness - the ignorance, be removed and light be there for the benefit of all races, religions, and nations.

"Let there be light, no darkness" our forefathers have said.

Appendix–A

Vritra

Vritra can be best understood in the book of Madbhagwat. It is said that if Veda is considered a tree, Madbhagwat is its fruit - sweet and ripe. The entire Madbhagwat contains the dialogues between Sukdeo, son of Rishi Vyasa, and the Pandav King Parikhsit, descendent of the five Pandavas. Parikhsit was cursed to die within a week. During a week the entire Madbhagwat was discussed between Sukdeo and King Parikhsit. The stories in Madbhagwat seem to have a deeper meaning and hidden principles, so they must be deciphered. The story related to Vritra is as follows:

> There was a king - Vidyadhar Chitra Ketu. He was very pious, generous and favorite of the Supreme, the Almighty. Once he was in an assembly of great saints, and scholars. In the assembly, Lord Shiva was sitting and his wife Parvati was on his laps and being caressed by her husband. Chitra Ketu did not like such behavior and he smiled sarcastically. Lord Shiva was smiling at Chitra Ketu's behavior, but Parvati got angry and cursed Chitra Ketu to be a demon in the next birth. Accordingly, Chitra Ketu was born as a demon in the house of Twasta and was named Vritra. In his infancy Vritra gained size and weight very fast. From his body emanated the luster of evening clouds

His hair, beard, moustache, were red like the color of heated copper and eyes were like the midday Sun. (Does this indicate the conditions of the death of a star?)

In war, Vritra swallowed all the weapons that Gods threw at him. (This is to be noted.) The defeated Gods approached the Supreme Almighty. He advised to make a special weapon out of the bones of Rishi Dadhichi. Indra came forward to kill Vritra with this weapon. During thez fight Vritra swallowed Indra along with his elephant; however, Indra was able to burst Vritra's stomach, cut his head and kill him.

In the above story, the following points are to be noted:

i) He was born out of Twasta—a Sun. In Vedic literature, the Sun is a star. Do the Rishis refer to dead stars?

ii) When Vritra was born his arms encircled the world around him? Does it mean Vritra was a comet?

iii) During the fight with Gods he swallowed all weapons and also swallowed Indra and his elephant. Does it mean Vritra was a Black Hole?

iv) Vritra was killed only when Indra went into his stomach.

It is for scholars of astronomy and astrophysics to decide whether Vritra was a black hole or not?

Appendix–B

Moon

The story is that once Moon went to the teacher of Gods, Brihaspati (Jupiter) for study. There this handsome Moon developed affairs with Brihaspati's wife, Tara, and fathered a child named Buddha (Mercury). For ownership of Buddha, Moon and Jupiter started fighting. Jupiter's claim was based on the fact that Tara was his wife while Moon claimed that he was the biological father of Buddha. Surya, being the king, took action and kept Mercury by his side.

From Astronomy point of view it seems that while planets and satellites were under formation, Moon came in proximity of a satellite of Jupiter and a chunk of Jupiter's satellite came out which started oscillating between the Moon, the satellite of Jupiter and the planet Jupiter. The force of Sun's gravity pulled the chunk which evenually settled in the vicinity of the Sun and is now called Mercury.

Appendix–C

Pusa

As per a story in Madbhagwat, the followers of Lord Shiva broke the teeth of Pusa, who is one of the Adityas. The word Pusa means nourisher. Pusa is considered the beneficiary rays of the Sun and giver of strength to humans. As Sun, Pusa also oversees the entire world and humans. With inspiration from Savita (another Aditya) he travels around. Prayer is made to Pusa for longevity and also for safe journey free from any difficulties and obstructions. This God Pusa has appeared 120 times in Ṛig-Veda, Pusa multiplies cattle and brings prosperity. Pusa has been described to be without teeth which may suggest that Pusa is harmless.

Appendix–D

Kamdeo

Kamdeo is the husband of Goddess Rati and is known as the God of Sex. The story is that once Kamdeo tried to induce sexual thoughts in Lord Shiva's mind while He was in meditation. This infuriated Lord Shiva and He opened his third eye. As a result, Kamdeo was burnt to ashes. When Kamdeo's wife Rati came to know about her husband's death, she prayed to Lord Shiva for pardon. Lord Shiva, the most generous Lord, pardoned him and said that Kamdeo will exist but without a body. So Kamdeo is called "Arang" which means without a body.

Appendix–E

Aswin Kumars

Lady Sangya, wife of Vivaswan (one of the twelve Adityas), once changed herself into a mare and went to Sun and gave birth to the twins Aswini on the earth. These twins learned medicine and as it would appear one was a physician and the other was a surgeon. They travelled fast and used air planes that have been mentioned in Ṛig-Veda.

For specialization they went to Rishi Dadhichi and requested the Rishi to teach them Brahma Vidya. The Rishi agreed and asked the twins to come some other day. In the meantime, Indra came and threatened Dadhichi not to give the knowledge of Brahma Vidya to the twins else the Rishi would be beheaded. When the twins came to know about the threat, they consoled the Rishi that they would replace the human head of the Rishi with a horse head and when Indra would cut horse head, his human head will be reattached. The Rishi agreed and taught the twins (1.119.9) that is why Brahma Vidya is now said "Ashwashira". It is not further known that whether Indra came to punish Dadhichi or not. After turns of events Dadhichi gave his bones out of which Vishwakarma made a superior weapon. But as per 1.84.14, after Dadhichi's death, his bones were found in a pond by Indra who made weapon of it and fought with demons.

Vishwakarma is the celestial architect and builder. He was the son of Angirasi and Vasu.

Dadhichi was son of Sukracharya. The chief priest and teacher of demons. According to another view, he was son of Atharwa and Shanti, who was daughter of a Rishi named Kadam. Indra taught Veda to Dadhichi and gave him the knowledge of Sanjivani (life saving medicine). Dadhichi gave up his life willingly and dedicated his bones so that a weapon could be made that eventually would be used by Indra to kill demon Vritra.

Appendix–F

Daksha

According to the sixth chapter of Madbahgwat there were sixty daughters of Daksha Prajapati. Daksha has been introduced in earlier pages. After projecting this universe, Brahma asked Daksha to create life on this earth. Daksha and his wife had ten thousand sons and sixty daughters.

Daksha married his 10 daughters with Dharma, 13 with Kashyap, 27 with Moon (27 constellations), 2 with Bhoot, 2 with Angira, 2 with Kusaksha, 4 with Daksharya Namdhari Kashyap.

> Dharma: His 10 wives were- Bhanu, Lamba, Kakoobh, Jami, Vishwa, Sandhya, Maruwati, Vasu, Muhurta, and Sankalpa
>
> Bhanu's son was Devreesham and his son was Indrasen.
>
> Lamba's son was Devreesham and his son was Meghgana.
>
> Kukubh's son was Saukat, his son was Keekat and Keekat's sons were proud Gods of all forts on this earth.
>
> Jami's son was Swarga and Swarga's son was Nandi.
>
> Vishwa's son was Vishwadev who was issueless.

Sandhya's son was Sandhyagama and his Arthasidhi.

Maruwati's has two sons, Marutwan and Jayant. Jayant is part of God Vasudev who is also called Upendra.

Muhurta's sons were proud Gods of Muhurts who give rewards according to their actions.

Vasu's had eight sons who are called Vasu. Their names are Drona, Prana, Dhruv, Arka, Agni, Dosh, Vasu, and Vibhavaen.

The wife of Drona is Abimati whose sons were the Gods of pleasure, fear and grief.

The wife of Prana, Urjaswati, gave birth to sons Sah, Ayu (Age) and Purojawa.

Dhruv's wife Dharani gave birth to sons Tarsa (Tarsa means Trishna meaning desire)

The Vasu named Agni was husband of Dhara who gave birth to son Draviranak.

Kritika's son Skandda was also born form Agni. Akanda's son was Vishakha.

Dosh's wife Sarvari gave birth to Shishmar, who is said to be God's Kala Avtar.

Vasu's wife Angirasi give birth to the celestial architect and builder Vishwakarma. Vishwakarma's wife Kruti gave birth of Chaksus Manu whose children were Visvadev and Sandhyagama.

Vivabasu's wife Usha gave birth to three sons, Vusta, Rochis, Atap. Atap son was Panchyam (Divas) due to whom all living beings are busy in their works.

Bhoot's wife, Daksha's daughter, Saroopa gave birth to millions of Rudragans. Out of these Rudras, eleven are the main. They are Raivat, Aja, Bhava, Bhim, Vam, Ugra, Urisakapi, Ajekpad, Ahirbudhanya, Vahuroot and Mahan.

Bhoot's second wife Bhoota gave birth to horrible Bhoot. All of them became councilors of the above eleven main Rudras.

Angiras' first wife Swadha gave birth to Nitreegana and the second wife of Angirs- Satee, accepted Atharwa - Angirasa Ved as her son.

Krisaksha's wife Achee gave birth to Dhumrakesh and his second wife Wishna had four sons Vedsheers, Deval, Vayun, Manu.

Taksharya Namdhari Kashyap's four wives were Vinata, Kadru, Patangi and Yamini.

Patangi gave birth to birds and Yamini gave birth to insects. Vinata's son was Garur, the celestial crane on whose back Lord Vishnu travels in air. Vinata's second son is Arun who is the charioteer of Lord Surya.

Moon's twenty seven wives are the twenty seven constellations. But Moon had maximum love for Rohini due to which Daksha cursed him and Moon became ill and weak and could not produce a child. After prayer to Daksha, Moon regained his health and two phases of Moon were added, but none of the ladies (constellations) gave any birth. As per Astrology, Moon is the lord of Rohini constellation which is in Taurus sign (Rashi) and hence Taurus sign is the house of exaltation of Moon.

Kashyap's thirteen wives were –Aditi, Diti, Danu, Kasta, Arista, Surasa, Iila, Muni, Krisvasa, Tamra, Suravi, Sarma, and Timi. All are said to be mothers of this universe and all life-forms.

Timi's children are creatures of water and dangerous tigers.

Saravi's children are buffaloes, cows and animals with two Khoor (hoofs).

Tamira's children are vultures, falcon, and other birds of prey.

Muni gave birth to Apsaras.

Krosvasa's children are poisonous creatures such as - snakes, and scorpions.

Iila's children are vegetation on the earth such as - trees, creepers.

Surasa's children were Yatudham (Demons).

Arista gave birth to Gandahrvas.

Kaste's children were one Khoor (hoof) animals such as - horse. Dhanu had sixty one sons, the important among them are- Dwimurdha, Sambour, Arista, Hayagriva, Vivawasu, Ayomukh, Shansushire, Swavanu, Kapil, Arun, Puloma, Brisparva, Ekchaktra, Annutpam, Dhumrakesh, Virupaksha, Viprachitya, and Durjaya.

Swavanu's daughter Suparva was married to Namichi and Brisparva's daughter Sharmistha was married to the mighty Yayati, son of Nahuns.

Danu's another son Vaishwanar had four daughters namely - Updanvi, Hayashir, Puloma, and Kalka.

Updhanvi was married to Hriyanaksha and Hayashire was married to Kratu.

As per Lord Brahma's desire, Kashyat married two daughters of Vaishwanar named above- Puloma and Kalka. From these two, sixty thousand fighter demons Paulom and Kalkeya were born. All were called Niwat Kawachi. They disturbed good actions. The great Pandav Arjun, killed them all to please his father Indra.

Viprachitya's wife Sinhika gave birth to one hundered and one sons. Out of them the large one is Rahu and the rest are Ketu. They are said to be malefic planets in Astrology.

Aditi - is the most honored lady. Her twelve sons are known as twelve Aditya - Vivaswan, Aryama, Pusa, Twasta, Savita, Bhog, Dhata, Vidhata, Varun, Mitra, Indra, and Trivikram (Vaman).

Vivaswan's wife Sangya gave birth to Sradhdeo (Vaivaswat) Monu, and daughter Yamini. This lady Sangya went to Sun in disguise of a "mare" and gave birth to the great twins Aswini Kumars.

Vivasan's second wife was Chhaya, who gave birth to two sons - Sameschar and Savani Manu and one daughter Tapati who married Somcharan.

Aryama's wife is Matrika - who gave birth to Charshana. the merits of Charshana.

Twasta's wife was Rachnana, sister of demons. Rachna gave birth to two sons, Sannivesh and the great Viswarup, who became Chief Priests of Gods after God's teacher Brihaspati left Gods when he was insulted by them.

In general, only eight Adityas (sons of Aditi), are mentioned instead of 12 as in Madbhagwat. From Astronomical considerations, twelve is a more logical number. The year is divided into twelve months. The hours of day and night are divisible by 12. The Vedic time for 24 hours is 60 Dand which is divisible by 12. In Vedic period came the concept of a circle representing the complete revolution of the earth around the Sun. The 365 days was reduced to 360 as this figure is divisible by all basic numbers except seven and so for early calculation purposes, 360 was a figure adopted for a circle.

The subject of geometry developed during the culture of continuous Yagya, where priest used to sit in turn for 24 hours facing east observing the planets. Very few people know that a rectangle is connected to all Gods, triangle to Shiva, and a pentangle to Shukra. Shukracharya was the Chief priest and teacher of demons, so Shukra (Venus) is not venerable with Hindus. But Venus being bright among all the planets got respect and regard in desert areas and hence got importance in Islam. In Islamic architecture, pentagon appears to be a significant element.

All these descriptions given in Madbahgwat cannot be or should not be brushed aside as fanciful tales. These descriptions indicate activities of nature and are very informative. A team of Sanskrit scholars and scholars of Physics, Biology, Botany, and Astronomy is required to understand and decipher these descriptions. For example, it is not clear as to why Sangya went in a disguise of a mare? Perhaps, a group of scholars can understand.

Appendix–G

Adityas

There are twelve Adityas among these twelve, Varun, Mitra, Bhag, and Aryama are very prominent. Mitra and Varun are generally together. Bhag occasionally joins with Savita. One form of Aditya signifies one month and jointly the twelve mean the year.

In diurnal variation, one form of Aditya signifies two hours. If one subdivides hour of Danda (Vedic time scale), the figure 12 goes a long way because - hour is divided into 60 minutes and one minute is 60 seconds.

Danda is subdivided into 60 Pala and one Pala in 60 Bipala. So if one considers one cycle of twelve Adityas, one hour means five cycles, each of 12 minutes. One can go deeper.

24 hours = 24x60x60 seconds. If divided by 12, it comes 7200 cycles of 12 seconds.

As regards these four—Bhag, Mitra, Varun and Aryama, the question is how to place them in a time frame. The general opinion is Mitra rules over day and Varun over night. However, it appears that Bhag and the other three, each, rule for six hours. Bhag is three hours before and after Sunrise. Next is Mitra, then Varun followed by Aryama. If Sunrise is at 6 a.m., then Bahg is 3 a.m. to 9 a.m., Mitra 9 a.m. to 3 p.m., and Varun 3 p.m. to 9p.m. and Aryama 9 p.m. to 3 a.m.

The scholars of Astronomy can opine on the above time schedule of the four Adityas - Bhag, Mitra, Varun, and Aryama.

If twelve Adityas are taken together, then one month is for one Aditya. If only four Adityas are to be considered then Bhag will stand for spring, Varun for rains, Mitra for agriculture and Aryama for severe winter.

Sanskrit scholars, astronomers and meteorologists together can interpret the Adityas and their significance.

Appendix–H

Jyotish Shashtra (Astrology)

From Veda came six Shastras. One of them is Jyotish (Astrology). In terms of classical science and applied science, Astrology is applied Astronomy.

This highly honorable subject astrology has suffered severe humiliation and has become a subject of satire. This is because Astrology has deviated from its real path.

This science is complementary to medical science. Astrology predicts when a disease will come but does not prescribe medicine. This is reverse of Medical Science which cannot predict disease years ahead but prescribes medicines.

Some astrologers deviated and made it a subject of success in election, predicting windfall etc. Over and above there had been no research for more knowledge.

Most of the people say that astrology is not scientific. In this context words of Richard P. Feynman, a Physicist and Nobel laureate is being quoted –

> "Everything is made of Atoms. This is the key hypothesis. The most important hypothesis in all of the biology for example is that everything the animals do, atoms do. In other words, there is nothing that living beings do that cannot be understood from the point of a view

that they are made of Atoms acting according to the laws of physics."

Are the Atoms on this earth absolutely independent or are they under the influence of stars, planets or satellites? Between the Sun and the Moon, one is very large and the other is very near (with respect to the earth). Among the planets, Jupiter is very large in size. In Veda all three (Sun, Moon, and Jupiter) are highly praised.

Astrology is an attempt to understand the effects of these celestial bodies on human beings. The agents must be atoms and molecules acting as per influence of celestial bodies.

Little attempt has been made in physics, or astronomy to assess what type of influence is exerted on terrestrial atoms by celestial bodies. It is taken for granted that atoms do not change and that atom remain uninfluenced but in this Universe nothing is independent.

In Astrology the sky is divided in twelve parts, starting from East to Zenith to West to Azimuth. Each part is for practical purpose, of thirty degrees. Each part is called House. The stars in the sky are grouped in twenty seven constellations called Nakshatras in Sanskrit. Each Nakshatra is divided in four equal parts. Each part, which is called pada (step), is of 360 divided by 27 times 4, which is equal to three degree twenty minutes. These twenty seven Nakshatras are within twelve Rashis that means each Rashi of thirty degree contains two and a quarter Nakshatras which is nine padas.

The twelve houses are fixed, the rashis rotate as the earth rotates and so do the Nakshatras. The Rashis which is rising at the eastern horizon at the time of birth is written in the first house which is called Ascendant (Lagna). Then all the Rashis are written in the fixed circles of houses in anti-clockwise manner. This gives the horoscope which is called Janma Kundali.

The horoscope is made in three manners, one is a circle, the other is rectangle and the third is in a square which is very popular.

In astrology Sun is called King, Moon is Queen, Jupiter is Guru (Master teacher), Mercury (Buddha) is prince, Mars (Mangala) is commander, Venus (Shukra) is Daitya Guru (Master of demons) and Saturn (Shanti) is the servant. Rahu and Ketu are mathematical points but in Astrology there are planets of menial types, malefic in nature.

The twelve houses have their individual significance. The main are written below:

Ist house: Brain, Appearance, Reputation, Health.

IInd house: Relations, Eyes, Accumulated money.

IIIrd house: Younger brother, Thyroid, Courage.

IVth house: Mother, Lungs, Landed Property.

Vth house: Children, Intelligence.

VIth house: Disease, Debts.

VIIth house: Opponents, Spouse, Cause of death.

VIIIth house: Death, Occult knowledge.

IXth house: Father, Religious attitude, Travel.

Xth house: Profession, Reputation.

XIth house: Earnings of wealth.

XIIth house: Bedroom pleasure, Confinement, Salvation, Long voyage.

Among the Adityas, four (Bahg, Mitra, Varun, and Aryama) are considered significant.

Bhag controls relations, eyes, brain, bedroom pleasure.

Mitra controls profit, gain, profession, reputation, father.

Varun controls death, opponents, cause of death, disease.

Aryama controls children, mother, younger brothers.

The above pattern shows the roles of these four Adityas in astrology. If the roles of the remaining eight Adityas are understood then each will get a house in the horoscope.

Appendix–I

Metres (Gayatri)

The Gayatri – "Om bhurbhuwa Swah, tat saviturvareṇyaṃ bhargho devasya dhīmahi | dhiyo yo naḥ pracodayāt ||" is being chanted since thousands of years. Gayatri is a metre. Rik Veda is in poems not in rhythm, but in various metres, called chhanda in Sanskrit. Among the six Shastras, emanating from Vedas is one Chhanda Shastra like Vyakaran (grammar, language), Nyaya (jurisprudence), Jyotish (astrology). Chhanda Shastra can be properly understood by scholars of music. In Veda the hymns have mantras and they are to be sung or even read in proper manner which means in the metre specified.

It is very shocking to hear priests chanting Gayatri in various manners. Different metres create different types of sound waves which create different types of effects in the listeners, humans and animals and even plants. In Ṛig-veda the fact that music affects plants has been mentioned.

There are approximately sixty types of metres, among them Gayatri is practically the one which is widely known. The Rishis the observers of nature and worshippers of various forces, energies, and departments of nature, have mentioned the subtleties of Gayatri and the other meters.

As per 1.161.23 the person who will realize Him who has established Gayatri on earth, Trist up in Antariksha, and Jagati in the sky, will attain immortality or Godhood. The Almighty created Pran from Gayatri, made Sam-Veda with groups of hymns, made sentences of Yajur-Veda by Trist up and by words of two or three "padas" made seven voices full of meters.

As per 10.130.4 and 5 Agni helped Gayatri, Vsnik (another meter) helped Savita, Som of Anusutup. Sun is with Uktho and Brihaspati with Brihati who gave words to Brihaspati. Mitra-Varun is associated with Virat and Tristup with Indra and Jagati got associated with many Gods.

So each and every Chhanda has a scientific meaning. For example Agni helps Gayatri. This clearly shows that by chanting Gayatri in proper manner one gets energetic. So Gayatri is useful in times of depression and fear. The chanting may be loud or in whisper what is important is that it should be in the proper manner (metre).

Brihati Chhanda develops capacity of brain to remember right words for right speech, Usnik and Anustur give mental rest. Scholars of music and physicists as well as scholars of medical science can jointly give proper meaning to the above combinations of Gods and Chhandas.

It is a point to discuss that when Ṛig-veda started with Gayatri "Agni melee...dhatman," then why it is not common like the Gayatri "Om bhurbhuwa...pracodayāt" which appears later in Yajur-Veda having its origin in Ṛig-Veda 3.62.10 which does not have the word "Om Bhurbhuwa swah" but commence with "tat saviturvareṇyaṃ bhargho devasya dhīmahi | dhiyo yo naḥ pracodayāt ||"

Moreover there are thousands of Gayatri chhandas then why the above "Om bhurbhuwa...pracodayāt" is selected. The reason should be the human being the children of the God Sun. His rising time is the time of arrival of many Gods and Goddesses like Aswins, Usha, Savita, and Bhag. All of them can be de-personified. This hour of Usha has many healthy rays beneficial to humans. The Rishis selected this God Savita and in his praise is the Gayatri - "Om bhurbhuwa Swah, tat saviturvareṇyaṃ bhargho devasya dhīmahi | dhiyo yo naḥ pracodayāt ||".

This Gayatri also means that Savita gives strength to brain and mind to think in right direction of life. Savita's rays are disease-fighting, worth absorbing by human bodies. Savita gives luster and divinity good for brain, mind, and health. As per 8.1.8, 8.1.10 and 8.16.9 special mention is to praise Indra by Gayatri.

Music came from the sound waves created by chirping of birds. It is said that the sound created at the time of solar flare, magnified fifty thousand times, seems as whisper of "Oum" (Om) which was said by Rishis as Anahat sound which means sound created without any beating of thumping. In Sanskrit "Hat" means hitting and "An" means without or none. This word (O U M) became sacred and used before chanting any hymns (Mantras). This "Oum" is personified as Brahma-Rudra-Vishnu and is the order in which He created. Brahma is all the rules (Personified) of nature. Rudra is the force and Vishnu is the space and the created matters. It seems now that the Rishis must have heard sound waves, in nature similar to the metres, Gayatri and Jagati. After much deliberation spanning years, the Rishis had decided to accept Gayatri as the most useful as it gives energy to humans and then they had started forming most of the hymns (Mantras) in Gayatri. Due to proximity and importance of Sun, "Om Bhurbuwa..." became household Gayatri.

From Gayatri came Tal Kaharva in Hindustani music which is Dha, Ge, Na, Ti, Na, Ka, Dhin, Na, Musicians can opine better.

Appendix–J

Various Types Of Marriages

Based on logic, convenience and for healthy children, Aryans had many rules and categories of marriages. The Ṛig-veda is the source of such rules etc. The various types of marriages are given below:

1. Marriage with the consent between the boy and the girl, for their pleasure, is called "Brahm."

2. Marriage of one's daughter with person qualified and expert in Yagya and while performing Yagya is called "Dev."

3. Marriage of one's daughter with a man who has paid for the marriage is called "Arya."

4. Marriage for the sake of propagating religious activities is called "Prajapatya."

5. Marriage after some payment to the boy and girl is called "Aasur."

6. Without auspicious time and without marriage rules, marriage with the consent of boy and girl is "Gandharva."

7. After fight, rape etc, the marriage is "Rakshas."

8. Marriage with a drunk, mentally retarded girl or forceful relation while the girl is in sleep is "Paishach."

Surrogate fatherhood is permitted under the "Niyog" system. Niyog is permitted for a woman whose partner is diseased, mad, or impotent. Niyog allows only one partner at a time for having a child. Through Niyog up to two children are permitted. Niyog is not allowed with siblings and certain relations for example, one can not have Niyog with wife of Guru, niece, daughter, daughter-in-law, mother, mother-in-law.

The man or woman should neither harm the partner nor displease the family and relatives of the partner. The essence of Niyog is for having good child and not pleasure.

The system of Niyog was adopted by the wives of Dasrath, father of Lord Ram. Dhritrastra, Pandu and Bidur were born under Niyog. This system was also adopted by the two wives of Pandu.

Appendix–K

Brahma's Day And Night

There are different interpretations of the duration of Brahma's day and night. For general understanding, there are four Yugas, namely, Satyug (Krityug), Tretayug (Trityug), Dwapar Yug and Kali Yug.

The duration in years of the Yugas are-

Satyug:	1728×10^3 years
Treta:	1296×10^3 years
Dwapar:	864×10^3 years
Kali:	432×10^3 years.

There is, however, controversy over meaning of the word "yug". According to Vedic scholars of the west, yug means generation and they prove it by quoting Ṛig-Vedic hymns. Some consider the meaning of yug to be conjunction and it is said that at the beginning of Kaliyug, the Sun and its planets were in conjunction. Some say that yug means a couple of day and night, or a couple of months or a couple of fortnights.

The general acceptance is that one yug refers to a period of time. In his book "The Arctic home in the Vedas" the great scholar and patriot, Bal Gangadhar Tilak, has written in detail about the controversy in meaning of the word yug and also the duration in years of yug and duration in days and nights of Brahma.

In his book "Rigvedadi Bhasya Bhoomika", Swami Dayanand Saraswati has avoided this controversy. According to him the duration in years of each yug is as given above.

The figure of the total years of the four yugas is 432×10^4 years. This is said as one "chatur yugi", indicating four. Seventy-one Chaturyigi make another unit of time called Manvantar. According to the great astronomer of India—Aryabhat, seventy-two Chaturyugi make one Manvantar.

The another unit of time is "Kalpa" which is equal to fourteen Manvantars. Also, one Kalpa is one day or one night of Brahma.

So Brahma's one year is 360x2 =720 Kalpas. And age of Brahma, is one year in this scale.

During Brahma's day, this creation exists and His night is period of deluge. Now the numerical value of Brahma's one day is:

$$71 \times 14 \times 432 \times 10^4 \text{ years}, \; 994 \times 432 \times 10^4 \text{ years}$$

If Aryabhat's view is taken then one day of Brahma is:

$$72 \times 14 \times 432 \times 10^4 \text{ years}, \; 1008 \times 432 \times 10^4 \text{years.}$$

Hence the difference is $(1008-994) \times 432 \times 10^4$years or $14 \times 432 \times 10^4$ years.

A middle path has been adopted by Vedic scholars as per which one day of Brahma is equal to $1000 \times 432 \times 10^4$ years.

So there are three figures

a) $994 \times 432 \times 10^4$ years

b) $1000 \times 432 \times 10^4$ years

c) $1008 \times 432 \times 10^4$ years.

Taking (b) as the reference point, the error is 0.6 percent and +0.8, both less than one percent. And for such astronomical calculations this error can be ignored.

So, after Brahma's death at his hundred years of age, there is nothing except Him—the Absolute. One may argue that when new Brahma is born there may be amendment in the laws of the previous period of Brahma, who knows? Only people like the Rishis, who realize the meaning of Infinity, can comment on existence and non-existence.

Appendix–L

Pioneers of Science and Technology

In ancient India, millenniums before the beginning of the Common Era, significant contributions were made in the fields of medicine, physics, cosmology, aviation technology, chemistry, and mathematics. Some of the pioneers and there contribution are given here:

Acharya Kapila (3000 BCE), known as the Father of Cosmology, explained the nature and principles of the ultimate soul, primal matter and creation. Also founded the Sankya philosophy.

Acharya Bharadwaj (800 BCE), contributed to Aviation technology and described three different types of flying machines-ones that fly over the earth between two locations; others that fly between planets; and the third that fly between different universe.

Acharya Sushrut (600 BCE), known as the Father of Plastic Surgery. Performed rhinoplasty, prescribed treatments for fracture and dislocation of limbs, and provided details of human embryology.

Acharya Charak (600 BCE), known as the Father of Medicine, gave the Charak Samhita, an encyclopedia of Ayurveda. He was a genius on anatomy, embryology, and pharmacology.

Acharya Kand (600 BCE), was the founder of the atomic theory, a pioneer in realism, and law of causation.

Acharya Patanjali (200 BCE), known as the Father of Yoga, prescribed the control of life-breath as a means to control body, mind and soul.

Nagarjuna (100 CE), was a pioneer in metallurgy and chemistry. He also contributed towards curative medicine.

Aryabhatt (476 CE), was a master Astronomer and Mathematician. Presented the heliocentric view, axis of the earth, and the shape of the earth. Presented formula for calculating the movement of planets and time of eclipses.

Varahmihir (500 CE), an Astrologer and Astronomer, wrote Panchsiddhant in the field of Astronomy and contributed to geography, constellation and botany.

Bhaskaracharya II (1114 CE), was a genius in Algebra, Arithmetic, and Geometry. His renowned works are Lilavati and Bijganita. He explains the force of gravity in his book Suyra Siddhant.

Bibliography

Colebrooke, H.T. *The Vedas,* Essay published in Asiatic Researches, 1805.

Daniken, Erich von. *Chariots of the Gods,* (Reprint), Berkeley Trade, 1999

Doniger, Wendy. *The Rig Veda* (Translation), Penguin Classics, 1981.

Doniger, Wendy. *Rig Veda- An Anathology of One Hundred and Eight Hymns.* Penguin Classics, 1983.

Hare, John Bruno. *Internet Sacred Text Archieve,* http://www.sacred-text.com

Knapp, Stephen. http://www.Stephen-knapp.com

Muir, John. *Metrical Translations from Sanskrit Writers with an Introduction, Many Prose Versions and Parallel Passages from Classical Authors. (Reprint),* Kessinger Publishing, 2004.

Pike, Albert. *Indo-Aryan Dieties and Worship As Contained in the Rig Veda.* Fork Press, 2007.

Ragogin, Z.A. *Vedic India as Embodied Principally in Rig Veda.* Kessinger Publishing, 2005.

Rolland, Romain. *The life of Vivekananda and the Universal Gospel.* 22nd Ed. Trio Process, 2005.

Roy, Raja Ram Mohan. *Vedic Physics.* Golden Egg Publishing, 1999.

Sharma, Sri Ram and Sharma, Bhagwati Devi (ed.). *RigVed Samhita (Hindi).* Brahmabarcharwa, Haridwar (U.P.), 1996

Shastri, J.L. (ed.), Griffith, Ralph T. H. *The hymns of the Rg Veda.* Motilal Banarasidass Publishers Pvt. Ltd., 1995.

Sri Aurobindo. *The Secrets of the Veda.*(3rd. ed.), Sri Aurobindo Ashram, Pondicherry, 1985

Sri Shankracharya. *Vivekchudamani* (Translated by Swami Madhwananda) 18th edition, Trio Process. 2005.

Swami Bhaskarananda. *The Essentials of Hinduism,* Sri Ramakrishna Math Printing Press, 1994.

Swami Vivekananda. *The Complete Work of Swami Vivekananda,* http://www.ramakrishnavivekananda.info

Wilson, H. H. *Ṛig-veda-Sanhitá: A Collection of Ancient Hindu Hymns,* Constituting the First Ashtaka, or Book, of the Ṛig-Veda ; etc. Translated from the Original Sanskrit. Wm. H. Allen and Co., London, 1886, Adamant Media Corporation, 2005.

Wilson, H.H. *The Rg-Veda : Hymns of the Rg-Veda.* (Reprint). 6 Vols, Satguru, 2002.

Notes

www.ingramcontent.com/pod-product-compliance
Lightning Source LLC
LaVergne TN
LVHW091259080426
835510LV00007B/325
* 9 7 8 1 9 3 5 1 2 5 2 2 8 *